GET YOUR LIFE TOGETHER(ISH)

A No-Pressure Guide for Real-Life Self-Growth

Julia Dellitt

Adams Media
New York London Toronto Sydney New Delhi

**adams**media

Adams Media
An Imprint of Simon & Schuster, Inc.
57 Littlefield Street
Avon, Massachusetts 02322

First Adams Media trade paperback edition
April 2019

Interior design by Katrina Machado

Manufactured in the United States of America

10 9 8 7 6 5 4 3 2 1

Library of Congress Cataloging-in-
Publication Data
Names: Dellitt, Julia, author.
Title: Get your life together(ish) / Julia Dellitt.
Description: Avon, Massachusetts: Adams
Media, 2019.
Identifiers: LCCN 2018055712 | ISBN
9781721400058 (pb) | ISBN 9781721400065
(ebook)
Subjects: LCSH: Self-actualization
(Psychology)
Classification: LCC BF637.S4 D448 2019 |
DDC 158.1--dc23
LC record available at
https://lccn.loc.gov/2018055712

ISBN 978-1-72140-005-8
ISBN 978-1-72140-006-5 (ebook)

Dedication

To my husband, Jared, for always believing in me.

Contents

Introduction

On a perfect day, I wake up around 5 a.m., meditate, and then sip on a glass of cold brew coffee while reading peacefully on the couch. I make it to work on time. I meet all my deadlines, pick up a happy toddler from daycare, and then practice yoga for an hour before breezily putting together a healthy dinner for the family. Before bed I floss, fold a load of laundry, and look at the number in my bank account with a satisfied smile. I fall asleep with every item on my to-do list checked off, ready to take on tomorrow.

KIDDING. I kid.

What life really looks like: I hit snooze on my alarm three times in a row before taking a rushed shower. I put on mascara while bargaining with my son to eat his waffle, then arrive five minutes late to a meeting. I delete the text appointment reminder from my dentist, rewrite an errand from two months ago in a messy planner, scramble to give the dog a walk after work, eat leftovers for dinner, and lay awake until 2 a.m. wondering if my student loan debt will follow me to the grave.

I'm willing to bet that you experience this type of disconnect too—this feeling of being a few steps behind the type of person you always wanted to be. Here's what you need to know: your life isn't an all-or-nothing problem to solve or thing to fix. You already know what is important, what's somewhat important, and what's not important to you at all. But you may want to make a few adjustments, and that's where *Get Your Life Together(ish)* can help.

In this book you'll find practical strategies to troubleshoot common lifestyle, health, relationship, finance, and career challenges. Each is broken down by difficulty level so you can experiment to figure out what works best for you based on what *you* need.

So if you're curious about cultivating a smidgen of self-improvement in your days, weeks, and months, and you want a permission slip to be authentically imperfect on the journey, this book is for you. So if you're ready, flip the page and let's start to get your life together—ish.

How to Use This Book

Using this book is easy and straightforward, and you can even customize it to fit your life and schedule. Pick a challenge, select a commitment level, and then implement it. For each challenge you'll find three difficulty levels—because, let's face it, on some days you may just want to make a small improvement, and on others you might be ready to grab the reins and make a lifestyle change. You can also use the Try This exercises as a way to implement each challenge, whether through an activity, a reflection, or a journal exercise.

Each difficulty level requires a different level of commitment:

- **Easy:** These challenges need almost no preparation, take very little time, and can be done as often as you like. If you have time to scroll through *Instagram*, you have time for this option.
- **Medium:** These challenges require a bit more preparation, and they may require you to commit to several days' worth of action to implement them fully, but overall they won't be too taxing on your everyday life. Try this type of challenge when you want to address a specific habit but also need some time to adjust and reflect before truly sticking with it for the long haul.
- **Hard:** These challenges will take the biggest commitment of your time and effort. They will require planning and forethought to implement, and are meant to be done when you are ready to make a new habit and incorporate it into your everyday life. With this one you're all in, and you're ready and willing to make a serious change. These challenges will also set you up to carry habits into the long term in order to potentially make a true change in your life.

This book will also highlight familiar roadblocks that may rise up as you begin each challenge and offer ways to push past the excuses that could get in your way. Like when you start and your brain immediately says, "Well, I'd love to do this, *buuuut*..." Trust me, it's going to happen, and I'm here to cheer you on as well as remind you to keep going.

Part 1

Lifestyle

This first part is intended to switch up certain elements of your lifestyle where you might be feeling a bit stuck. People often talk about making their life "better," and while that word is incredibly subjective, you can indeed find ways to make your life a little bit better using some of these strategies.

In this part you'll learn how to become more of a morning person, get shit done, start journaling, and walk into the week with a positive attitude. It will discuss why repairing your possessions can lead to a sense of pride and ownership, why you need to avoid the busy trap at all costs, and why you absolutely have time to read a book. You'll also find tips for controlling your screen time addiction, making fun a regular part of your existence, and finding peace with what you like and dislike—so you can focus on being who you are and living a life you're proud of.

CHALLENGE #1:
Wake Up Earlier

As a kid I l-o-v-e-d sleeping in. Nothing beat the feeling of snuggling up under the covers, surrounded by pillows, with the satisfaction of knowing I could lie around and rest to my heart's content. Well, until my dad walked into my bedroom, flipped on the lights, and yanked the sheets off my body while singing his "Good morning, good morning, to you, to you" song at full volume. I would complain; he'd tell me that I could sleep when I'm dead.

Now, as an adult, I can understand where he's coming from—not the whole dying part, but the fact that mornings are completely underutilized. While working full-time after the birth of my first child, I swiftly realized how much I could accomplish in the wee hours of daylight, before the rest of the family woke up. I started tweaking my routine every week to figure out how to roll out of bed with a semi-decent attitude and the motivation to stay upright. It's true you'll have to ignore all those things that will try to lure you back to the coziness of your bed: the "Just five more minutes" mentality, a soft pillow, a dark room, your partner or anyone else (including pets) still sleeping soundly in that same bed, a quiet house, your pajamas, realizing you don't *really have to* get up quite yet, feeling tired, closing your eyes, any hesitation whatsoever.

But if I can do it, anybody can. Here's how.

WAKE UP FIFTEEN MINUTES EARLIER TODAY

The first part of this challenge requires you to wake up just fifteen minutes earlier than your normal time. It may seem like a huge feat if you are not usually a morning person, but I promise it will be worth it. How? You are going to bribe yourself. That's right, I'm serious; bribe your poor tired self.

For me, getting up and staying up when my alarm went off required one reward: buying coffee at my favorite little shop on the way to work. I even wrote it down on a piece of paper next to my phone so I would see it when the Alarm Gods called. For you, it might be something else, but pick something that you *really* enjoy, that would be a delight on a weekday, and use that as your motivation.

Then put your phone, or whatever you use for an alarm clock, across the room so you have to physically move your body and take a few steps to shut it off. Set the time for just fifteen minutes earlier than you would normally wake up. Do not, I repeat, *do not* get all ambitious here. If you tend to get up around 6:30 a.m., set your alarm for 6:15 a.m. It might sound like too small of a change to be effective, but trust me, it works. And after you do it once, you'll discover it's really not that big of a deal and maybe this morning stuff isn't so bad.

WAKE UP THIRTY MINUTES EARLIER EACH DAY FOR A WEEK

Why would you want to wake up thirty whole minutes earlier? The payoff here is that you use those thirty extra minutes to do something just for you—something you like but never quite have time for in your day. You could make a nice egg sandwich for breakfast, read the last few pages of a book you keep trying to finish, journal for a few minutes, stand in the living room and enjoy the view from your window, put on a face mask, watch the news, or just sit outside with a cup of coffee. It doesn't have to be anything fancy; this is just about taking those thirty minutes to get back a little peace in your life. You'll find that even after a week, you'll crave this "me time" and you won't mind waking up earlier to get it.

Here's how you do it: you have a little flexibility here, but essentially pick a wake-up time that's about thirty minutes earlier than your norm, enough to feel like you're showing up differently but not a change that feels too hard. Remember, you're not trying to turn yourself into a morning person for life, so the pressure is off.

These thirty minutes will become a little window of time carved out just for *you*. Rather than viewing waking up early as an annoying intrusion, consider what it would feel like to start your day with the knowledge that you *at least* did one thing for yourself.

WAKE UP EARLY EVERY DAY FOR A MONTH

This hard version of the challenge doesn't require you to wake up hours earlier than your usual time (in fact, you can keep the thirty-minute increment of the medium challenge), but the key to this challenge is maintaining the habit. Sure, it's not so bad waking up thirty minutes earlier for a week, but can you make it a whole month and turn it into a new habit? This is where your determination will really come into play.

To accomplish this challenge, I suggest using the same wake-up time as before (the thirty minutes earlier than usual), but you can also experiment with waking up forty-five to sixty minutes earlier if you feel daring. The bigger the space between your current routine and your ideal routine, the harder it's gonna be to stay consistent—don't say I didn't warn you. Then again, just like before, make yourself a list of incentives for waking up earlier. What are the things that will make this waking up worth it for you?

The key here is the longevity of this challenge. If you can make it one month waking up earlier, you will have started a new habit that will be easier to maintain. It will not only become part of your normal routine to wake up earlier, but you'll have the added benefit of using the extra time to do what you want to do and get your day off to a better start.

TRY THIS

Wake up an hour earlier than you normally do for an entire month and track how much you're able to accomplish in this extra time. Write down all the things you got done that probably would have been still sitting on your to-do list if you had decided to hit the snooze button. Then reward yourself for meeting this goal, and play around with how you might carry your early wake-up time forward as a regular morning habit.

Get Shit Done

Part of being an adult means doing a lot of little errands that are, to speak generously, time-consuming and draining. Things like getting your oil changed, making appointments, returning purchases to the store, filling out paperwork, going to three different stores for five different items, returning a phone call or text, figuring out why your credit card bill is off by $2—you get it. And if you don't stay caught up on your adulting to-do list, then you'll likely find yourself either completely behind in life or swapping potentially relaxing weekends for traffic and tasks. Nobody really told me how relentless all this extra work of being a grownup would be, and some months I end up rewriting the same list over and over in my planner, but it never seems to get checked off. Then, when I finally take care of whatever it is, I feel immensely better and wonder why it took me so freaking long to follow through.

Now, whenever I'm procrastinating on life's various assignments, I remind myself of that feeling of being done—and I've learned a couple of tricks to help motivate myself over the mental hump of "Ugh, I don't wannaaaaa."

DO THAT ONE SMALL THING YOU'VE BEEN PUTTING OFF FOREVER

Picture this scenario: you walk into your home and immediately notice a pile of clean, crumpled laundry. You think about folding it, then you tell yourself you'll fold it later. You step over those clothes, oh, about ten times that evening, all the while feeling annoyed that the laundry exists in the first place, wondering why you didn't fold the clothes after they first came out of the dryer because now everything is all wrinkly. Or maybe you're great at folding laundry, and instead it's hard for you to follow through on something else, like picking up clutter or emptying the recycling bin. For me, it's mail. The other week I needed to mail a donation from an event I attended. I wrote the check, sealed it with a stamp...and left it on my counter for two weeks. It's not like the mailbox is far away, either; it's literally at the end of my driveway, and putting anything in there takes about two minutes round-trip. Here's the funniest part, in my opinion: every time I saw that envelope, I thought about how I really needed to put it in the mailbox. I spent priceless mental energy lamenting this tiny task on my to-do list when it would've taken me a fraction of that time to just *do* it!

If you're feeling overwhelmed by everything on your plate, then start by checking just one thing—ideally, a super simple, "You've been meaning to do it anyway" thing—off your list in a given day. Once you've done that, you can take it a step further and take care of a few more. Again, make it easy on yourself—pick the ones that don't require three phone calls, four stops, or any paperwork whatsoever. Write them down, because the act of writing them down will add a little edge of commitment to following through, and then give yourself the option of completing one per day or using a block of time in the week to do them all at once. The how and when doesn't actually matter, just the task itself, so do what's best for you and check those items off your list.

DON'T BREAK THE CHAIN

Whenever I accomplish a single task, I feel pretty proud of myself, and I've learned to use that momentum to keep the trend going. For example, if your goal is to drink one gallon of water each day, write a thousand words for your novel, or play with your kids for a half hour every evening after work, it's easier to be successful if you keep it going versus starting and stopping.

Here's how it works: start with a visual that allows you to see and mark your progress. You can use a basic paper calendar, your planner or journal, a whiteboard, an app, whatever. Next, every time you accomplish your daily goal, mark it accordingly. You can put a big red X over that day in your calendar or check a box to note that you made it happen. Now aim to create a chain that doesn't break—a string of X's or completed tasks in a row—and don't let any non-X days ruin the mojo. When you track your progress in a visual way, it not only serves as motivation to get shit done but also indicates how far you've come.

MAKE A LIST OF *ALL* THE THINGS YOU NEED TO DO, AND THEN DO THEM

DIFFICULTY LEVEL:

HARD

I'm a list person. I love making lists, and I love crossing things off a list even more. But I also know the feeling of looking at a very long list and thinking, *Ew, no.* Sometimes putting it all on paper doesn't motivate you to accomplish more; it just makes you want to hide under a rock until some other responsible person steps in. Yet there's something to be said for knowing what you're up against—so if you truly want to get a grip on all the little things that need to be done in life, make a list.

It's best to do this exercise at the start of a month, simply because it's a fresh start, but you can do this for any thirty-day period too. First (as motivation), think ahead to a month from now and the feeling of "Hallelujah, I am winning the Game of Life" that you will be experiencing. Next write it all down, from the easy "buy dog food" to the complicated or time-consuming "renew driver's license." Then create a game plan and work your way through the list during the month. Don't worry about whether or not you'll get it all done, either. From my experience, you'll likely do much more than you ever intended, just from making a monthly list and then slowly but surely removing a few items from that list every week.

TRY THIS

Make a list of all the things rattling around in your brain that you've been meaning to do, no matter how big or small. Pick a short time frame to power through as much of this list as possible: take a day off work one week, plan for an afternoon on a given weekend, or even reserve just one hour where you completely focus on this list. Don't get sidetracked by other miscellaneous chores or errands, and don't put things off for when you have more time or energy. Just muscle through and complete what you can within in the set time frame, and then rejoice in the fact that you got some shit *done*, my friend.

CHALLENGE #3:
Start a Journal

Growing up, I always had four or five notebooks lying around, usually gifted from one of my parents with an inspirational saying on the front cover, and I wrote in the first ten pages or so before getting bored and discarding my journal for Beanie Babies or the new Boyz II Men cassette tape. Even though I wanted to be a writer when I grew up, the act of writing out my day-to-day thoughts and feelings seemed tedious at best. But in college and my early twenties, as life became more complex, journaling offered a safe space. I struggled with body image, relationships, perfectionism, and people-pleasing, among other issues, and my journal gave me permission to lay it all bare. I could be my worst self, or my most confused self, or my most self-involved self, and nobody would know but me. And when I returned to some of those entries months or years later, I saw bits and pieces of the person I was trying to be, aha moments that later took shape in a meaningful way, and most of all, a collection of memories that I would've otherwise forgotten.

We live in a digital world where everything is on the cloud or captured in real time for a tailored audience—so there's something valuable about journaling just for yourself, for no other reason than to chronicle a slice of time in your life that won't be later forgotten. The best part? There aren't any rules to journaling. You can start anytime, anywhere, at any age.

WRITE FOR FIVE MINUTES

People who want to journal, but don't, are often tripped up by one of the following mind-sets: (a) OMG, what if I write something totally dumb or pointless, (b) I don't have time for this, (c) I need to go to the store and buy a fancy leather notepad, or—my personal favorite—(d) I'm not a "good" writer. Let's dismantle each one, shall we?

First, nobody is going to read what you wrote except for you, and that's only if you want to. You probably *will* write something dumb or pointless, but who cares? You're not Tolstoy; you're a human trying to practice putting thoughts on paper. Second, you have five minutes, so stop making excuses. Third, don't fall into the trap of needing to spend money before embarking on any self-improvement efforts! All you need is a blank piece of paper. Finally, the writing police are not around the corner, waiting to lock you up for being mediocre. You do not need to be a published writer with a degree in creative writing for permission to write or for your words to matter.

All you have to do is write for five whole minutes. You can spend the whole time complaining about how your mom pissed you off the other day, or how you miss your ex, or how your boss smells. You can spend these five minutes noting everything you're thankful for: a beautiful day, strong cocktails, enough money to pay your rent or mortgage, someone to hug, dental insurance. Or you can write "I have nothing to say" over and over again. It doesn't matter. Set the timer and go.

TRY THIS

Find a piece of paper or open your computer to a blank document. Using your phone or a kitchen timer, set the clock to count down five minutes. Then start writing. The key here is to write the entirety of the five-minute period. If you find yourself glancing at the clock, or staring off into space worrying about "what to write," or crossing things out and hitting the delete button every time you put some words down, simplify. Let it be truly easy; write literally *whatever* pops into your brain until the timer goes off.

WRITE FOR FIVE MINUTES A DAY, THREE DAYS THIS WEEK

Building upon the easy challenge, aim to write for the same amount of time, but do so repeatedly throughout your week—otherwise you're going to end up like me at age sixteen with too many unfinished journals. Instead you're trying to form a habit, which will take a little longer. This is when the writing part will start to feel boring and dull, like homework, and you're likely to encounter some resistance in the form of "I don't know what to say." And *that's* when most people quit.

I'll share a secret with you: the vast majority of worthwhile choices in life are not incredibly sexy, particularly the ones where you have to put in repeated effort. I know—blah. That reality irritates those of us who live in this hyper-connected, always stimulated world...which is, um, all of us. Journaling is no different. You sit there for a couple of seconds or minutes, and you mostly think about the fact that you're bored and you could be doing all these other things and writing is pointless anyway. Then you get tired of that line of thinking, and your mind starts to wander over to one thought that snakes its way to the front: a reflection from the day prior, a question you want the answer to, the realization that you're quite tired or sad or grateful or content. Any one of those thoughts is worth exploring and will probably stoke your interest, but you can't get to that point without slogging through the "I'm so bored" phase. You won't notice how you feel, or what's going on with your inner self, unless you consistently pause to make space for those observations.

WRITE FOR FIVE MINUTES EVERY DAY FOR A MONTH

You see where I'm going with this, right? You're utilizing the same structures and habit-forming behaviors as before, just over a longer period of time. You will 100 percent have days where you're not feeling it and you can't remember why you even cared about writing on a daily basis in the first place. Stick with the five-minute plan because, again, you can do anything for five minutes. If you have time to watch an episode of your favorite show, look at social media, talk on the phone, take a shower, work out, etc.—then you have time to write for five gosh-darn minutes.

Throughout the month look for patterns of thought or behavior—meaning that if every time you sit down to write, you immediately jump up to do the dishes or walk the dog or rearrange a closet, then maybe that's a red flag you miiiiiight be avoiding something deep down. Or you just really dislike journaling, in which case, scrap it as a goal after the month is over. Perhaps every entry alludes to your desire to quit your job, or the fact that you're ready to get engaged, or you wish you owned a cat, or you want to try a capsule wardrobe. Again, it doesn't necessarily matter *what* you notice, but you will probably notice *something* in relationship to how you're feeling, a direction you'd like your life to go, or a change you might need to make.

CHALLENGE #4:
Skip the Sunday Scaries

On Sunday nights I used to feel an immense sense of dread—obligated, mildly depressed, unproductive—like everything ahead was going to be challenging and awful. I would toss and turn in bed, watching the minutes tick by, and ultimately wake up the next day exhausted and in a cranky mood, as though my predictions had come true. Now, for the most part, I feel rested and ready. I look forward to Sundays as a soft entrance to a fresh new week, and when the following day arrives, I'm someone who actually *doesn't* have a case of the Mondays.

How did this happen? Several years ago, I decided to change my attitude around the beginning of the week. I turned Sundays (or even Saturdays, if I really got ahead of the game) into organizational days, with a heavy dose of rest, and Mondays consequently shifted to "do the bare minimum" days. As a result, I no longer experienced the so-called Sunday scaries on a regular basis. I looked forward to the week ahead with minimal stress. Here's how you can do the same.

FIGURE OUT WHAT YOU NEED AND TAILOR YOUR SUNDAY TO IT

DIFFICULTY LEVEL:
EASY

In many religions Sunday is a sacred day of rest, but regardless of your spiritual affiliation or beliefs, and in the loosest, most secular interpretation of the phrase, it's an invitation to regroup, reset, and refresh your mind, body, and spirit. Sundays are not, as modern culture would suggest, an extra day to push yourself to the limit. Once I started paying attention to how I handled the transition from weekend to week, the difference in a red light versus green light mind-set became incredibly clear. Sundays spent working—going balls to the wall and rushing around—ultimately wore me out, and then I walked into Monday with an emotional (and sometimes physical) hangover of feeling drained. Conversely, Sundays spent sleeping in, being outside, indulging in creativity, and connecting with friends and family made me feel energetic, restored, and supported.

If you're not sure where to begin, then start with what you know, which is probably what's *not* working. For me, that involved eating a ton of junk food, watching hours of TV alllll day long, looking at social media for too long, getting no fresh air, checking work email, and staying up too late. What did work: the opposite of everything just listed, plus a deliberate effort to be proactive about the week ahead. I would glance through my planner and calendar, and think about which days were going to be busier than usual and which ones had more freedom, where I'd need to hustle or back off.

Think about what you need on Sunday, not what you have to do or should do, and make adjustments based on what choices would actually make your Monday feel a little bit easier.

LOOK AT YOUR WEEK AHEAD AND CATEGORIZE THE DAYS

People tend to ask me how I "do it all." Two responses: I don't even *try* to do it all, and also, time management. I strive to be as efficient as possible, at least in terms of managing my top priorities. I don't work nonstop or live a ridiculously structured life with no wiggle room, but I do categorize my days.

At the beginning of each week, I look at each day to determine how much I have going on and how that might impact my energy levels, health, family, or capacity. For example, if I see that Tuesdays and Wednesdays are full of meetings at the office but the rest of the week is pretty clear, then that means I need to take it easier on myself at home toward the front of the week. Similarly, most nights I dive into writing assignments after my son goes to bed, but at least a few times a week, I need to let myself off the hook so I don't completely crash and burn. That's why on Monday nights I intentionally do whatever I can to wind down in a way that's relaxing or full of self-care; I don't do anything strategic or creative on Mondays.

Determining the mix between hustling and backing off is key, and on Sundays I've found value in looking at the week ahead with a perspective of, "Okay, based on everything I know, what do I need to be successful and sane?" You can do the same.

TRY THIS

Categorize your week. Maybe, for you, Mondays are "productive" days and Fridays are "creative" days. Or perhaps you know Tuesdays and Thursdays tend to be go-go-go, so those are "green light" days, and the other days of the week are more "red light" (for backing off or downtime) or "yellow light" (for slow and steady). Look at your calendar for the week, and mark each day accordingly so you can get into the right frame of mind.

SET A GOAL FOR THE END OF THE MONTH, AND USE EACH SUNDAY TO HELP YOU GET THERE

Jen, a friend of mine and Chicago-based life coach, introduced me to a unique way of setting goals. Rather than picking goals and visualizing working toward them, she recommends setting your goals and then working backward through mini weekly targets to guide you toward the greater goal. Similarly, you can use the skills you've just built around being intentional with your Sundays and Mondays to achieve the same thing.

Take running: let's say that at the end of next month, I really want to get to a place where I'm running three times a week. Maybe this is a long-held goal of mine, but I feel like I "never" have time, so every week I end up making excuses for why I'm not running or it seems too hard. Instead of vaguely saying to myself, "Gee, I want to run three times a week," I decide I want to run twelve times by the end of the month, and work backward using my Sundays and Mondays. Every Sunday I might look at the week ahead and figure out which days are best for running twenty minutes. I schedule it out. I give it a go that week. Then the next week, I do the same thing—it's Sunday, I look at my week ahead, I'm intentional about how I'm spending my Sunday in order to be successful on Monday, I make adjustments based on whatever I need, and then I do it two more times. When the end of the month arrives, it's not a knee-jerk moment of "Oh wait, it's already summer and I didn't even try to run" or "Shoot, I only ran once!" I'm able to hold myself accountable.

You can apply this perspective to any goal, because when you treat the beginning of the week like a fresh start rather than a thing to be avoided at all costs, you're more likely to garner traction on whatever you're trying to accomplish.

CHALLENGE #5:
Repair Instead of Replace

Nowadays it is insanely easy to throw out what's broken or not working in favor of buying a low-cost replacement that arrives in forty-eight hours in a box on your doorstep. I love my Amazon Prime, but I also grew up with parents and grandparents who appreciated resourcefulness. If something didn't work, then you tried to fix it before doing anything else; if you didn't know how to repair it, you learned. My in-laws are the exact same way: whatever they don't know how to do, they teach themselves to know for next time. Which, in the age of *YouTube*, isn't hard since there's a how-to video for almost anything and everything.

That mentality expands to cleaning and maintenance too. For example, my dad takes obsessive care of his vehicles, to the point where it's a running joke in our family. He washes his car by hand, vacuums the floorboards every week, and waxes the paint to buff out any marks or scratches. He changes the oil on time and rotates the tires regularly. He'll even park in the rear of a parking lot just so nobody will accidentally door-ding him. The result? His cars last a long time. To him, a car isn't a thing you discard or trade out the second it breaks down or gets dirty or you're ready for a new model. It's something you own, and you're responsible for caring for the things you own, especially if you want them to last longer.

IDENTIFY ONE POSSESSION THAT YOU CAN REPAIR AND FIX IT

Even if you're the type to take excellent care of every possession you own, at some point a material item will break. And then you have three options: fix it, replace it, or throw it away. Sometimes you don't have much control over the situation; you might attempt to fix or replace it before realizing the only option involves the trash can. For the purpose of this challenge, your job is just to notice and identify one thing you own that needs to be repaired in some way: the desk stapler that always jams, the undone hem of your favorite pair of pants, a cracked Tupperware container. If you're anything like me, you've probably noticed this item for a little while now but didn't take direct action. Instead of fixing the stapler, you use a paper clip. Instead of hemming the pants, you wear a different pair of jeans. Instead of pitching the container, you sigh over the way it leaks every time you bring your lunch to work. None of these are a "big deal" individually, but separately each functions as a little inconvenience that hinders your productivity, affects the way you present yourself in the world, and even creates actual messes.

TRY THIS

Walk around your home, and every time you see something that could be fixed or improved in a minute or two, take care of it right then. Squeaky door? Grab the WD-40. Broken heel on your favorite pair of shoes? Put them in your car to be taken in for repair the next day. Busted refrigerator shelf? Order a new part online. The point is to immediately do *something* to address the things in your line of sight that need fixing, rather than ignoring them.

MAKE A LIST OF ALL YOUR ITEMS THAT NEED TO BE REPAIRED, AND DETERMINE WHAT YOU CAN DO YOURSELF AND WHAT REQUIRES EXPERT HELP

After we bought our first home, our fridge started leaking—not a ton, just enough to make a puddle on the floor that needed to be mopped up a few times a week. We poked around, trying to determine the source of the leak. No luck. We talked about calling a repairman, and then it fell to the bottom of the to-do list. In the meantime, we put an old towel at the base of the fridge. Friends who came over for dinner asked, "What's with the towel?" and we replied, "Oh, our fridge leaks sometimes." Additionally, an interior shelf of the fridge broke around the same time, crowding containers of jam and jars of minced garlic. (First-world problems, for sure.) We went on like this for months, until one day enough was enough. My husband looked up the make and model of the fridge, went to the website of the company, and ordered a replacement shelf for, like, thirty bucks. I called our home warranty company and put in a request for maintenance, and a repairman came out the next week to replace a coil related to the freezer. Boom: corrected shelf that opened up plenty of space, and no more water on the floor.

These are domestic examples, but it can be anything—a door that doesn't shut right, a game missing half the pieces, pens empty of ink. Notice whatever isn't working, particularly items front and center within your day-to-day routine, and tally them up. Then figure out if it's something you can fix (buy new pens!) or you need to call in an expert (save up for a shoe repair visit!).

GET RID OF WHAT YOU'RE NOT WILLING TO REPAIR

I am amazed at the number of semi-broken or nonfunctioning things people own "just in case." Just in case what? In case you might want the replacement button to a pair of pants that used to fit you a decade ago? In case you decide to use the mini Crock-Pot with the missing lid, for all the hot dips you never make? In case you need an extra computer cord from 1990? No—pitch it. Get rid of it. Accept the fact that some of your possessions will break or stop working and you're not obligated to keep them around for your great-great-grandkids. If it's no longer useful, you don't have a need for it anymore, it doesn't match your lifestyle or preferences, and most importantly, *you don't care enough to actually repair it*, get rid of it. Donate, recycle, throw it away, have a yard sale—if you're not going to take care of it in the next month in order to use it, then rid yourself of it. I'm looking at you, $10 flip-flops with a broken toe strap that I wore into the ground; I am no longer saving you for Future Me, because Current Me isn't even interested in giving you a second chance at life. Let go of the emotional baggage that comes with clutter so you can move along.

CHALLENGE #6:
Stop Being "So Busy"

Busy is a badge of honor, one we've all presented proudly when someone asks us how we are. Here's the thing, though—you are not special for being busy. In fact, I'm willing to argue that being "ugh, so busy!" mostly acts as a distraction for your feelings and a blocking device for true connection. And I promise I'm not lecturing you. I've been there; I understand the comfort in a fully packed calendar and a ready-made explanation at your hip. I've also learned firsthand that busy never ends, whether it's self-imposed or dictated by other people or circumstances. If you let being busy run your life, that will always be your norm, and you'll forget how to do things like be bored, be still, be relaxed, or even be uncomfortable. If every conversation revolves around how busy you are, there's never an opportunity to dive past the small talk for dialogue with more depth.

PRIORITIZE YOUR TO-DO LIST

You can probably think of at least one thing you're doing right now where you're not really sure *why* you're doing it. It makes you feel a little heavy, irked, committed—and yet it's still pending in your mind as a Thing to Be Done. Let me ask: is it really necessary that you do this thing?

Of course, there are certain choices you have to make due to loyalty, professionalism, and your own value system. It's not always about you and what you want, and paying attention to the grander scheme of things or the greater good is vital. But if any of your "shoulds" today cause the slightest sense of dread, pay close attention, and then pick one thing to let go of.

Try this little experiment: write down every moment this week where you said yes and later felt regretful. Be specific and honest with yourself about the reason(s) why; don't worry about any judgment or what you might do next. Just think about why you said yes. If it helps, try to frame it as an either/or question to be answered: did I want her to view me as the type of friend who is game for drinks on a weeknight, or did I truly want to see her and reconnect? It's okay if your answers feel a little icky or embarrassing or surprising. Until you can articulate what creeps into your psyche and pushes you to say yes out of ego or obligation or fear, you won't be able to discern the difference between when you want to do something and when you feel like you should.

You aren't doing anyone any favors by crowning yourself a "yes" martyr. If you feel like your day is filled with "shoulds" instead of things you truly *want* to do, then it's time to start trimming the fat.

DON'T CHECK YOUR PHONE TODAY

Moving away from the busy trap isn't just an exercise in learning to say no; it's a chance to make space for yourself through thoughtful boundaries. Doing this might feel a little selfish or strange, but it is a necessary act of self-care. Not checking your phone for a day releases you from the unnecessary obligations and often self-imposed commitments it generates.

This challenge is all about you reclaiming your time and clarifying your priorities. It may be more difficult for some people than others, and to accomplish it, you may need to create some rules such as creating a password for family members to use if there is an emergency, only reading emails from work on your current project, and so on.

Putting yourself and your priorities first is not an easy task, however, and I respect the people in my life who model this behavior. My friend Jenny, for instance, doesn't check her phone during the day; she is intentional about her priorities, and doesn't rearrange her life or schedule at the sound of a text message.

So much of our busyness is self-imposed by the desire to look good, appear useful, avoid disappointing others, or trying to seem like a good friend or nice person. None of those are good reasons to do *anything*. For one day put your phone and the busyness it generates aside, and just focus on what you need or want to do. The world—and all its pressure and commitments—can wait.

TRY THIS

It's common to underestimate how much time you spend on your phone or how often you pick it up to "check" something. That's why downloading a free app, like Moment, can help you see exactly how much time you spend on your phone each day and what you spend those minutes (or hours) doing. It can be eye-opening to see how much of your day you spend looking at things on your phone—when you could be using this time for other things in your life.

SCHEDULE "ME TIME"

DIFFICULTY LEVEL:
HARD

Busy people are boring. It's true. If all you have to talk about in your life is how busy you are, then what are you really accomplishing? A life of rushing places and scheduling commitments sounds pretty meaningless and empty, not to mention the toll it takes on your mind, body, and spirit. It's time to take back your life from the busyness and schedule time for what you truly want to do. That's right—a little "me time."

Time alone to do what you want to do is so important for mental health; it reboots your brain, improves concentration, helps you unwind, and enhances your relationships. Yet so many people put it on the back burner in favor of spreading themselves thin for the benefit of others. It's time to take back your me time. Schedule a monthly date with yourself and then do something you want to do: get a massage, write a letter, watch your favorite TV show, take a hike, or whatever it is that makes you feel relaxed and happy.

Taking care of yourself is what will sustain you and give you the energy to take care of all the other responsibilities you have. Want to be a better worker, parent, spouse, child? Then take some time for yourself instead of spending all your time in busy tasks for others. Make time for you.

CHALLENGE #7:
Read More

When I mention my reading habits to friends and acquaintances—novels before bed, the newspaper on Sunday mornings, a magazine in the bath, long-form articles online during my lunch break—I usually get a reaction like this: "Must be nice! I wish I had time to read." It used to make me feel defensive and guilty. Maybe I wasn't spending my time properly? Should I be reading so much? But I soon realized a reaction like that actually had nothing to do with me; the person replying either had no interest in reading for fun or was envious of my ability to do so.

I've been on both sides of the coin. Before I had children, I read all the time, but once my little ones arrived, I had to reevaluate reading as a priority. For a while I had no interest in it; sleep inched up much further on the priority scale. But eventually I missed reading and craved a way to make it happen. I knew I wouldn't be able to return to my pre-kid mode of consuming literature, but I also didn't want to spend the next twenty years of my life not ever reading anything, either. Reading is no longer an hours-long indulgence of sitting on the couch with a cozy blanket, book in hand. I now have to take advantage of smaller pockets of time: fifteen minutes there, thirty minutes here. That's what works for me, and makes it possible to keep reading within the constraints of my actual life.

You have to decide if reading for pleasure is important to you, and if it is, here's how you can make it work.

CARVE OUT TEN MINUTES TO READ WITHOUT INTERRUPTION

I'll be blunt: if you have ten minutes to look at social media, you have ten minutes to read. If you truly, truly don't have ten minutes in a twenty-four-hour period, then start with five minutes, or even two. When people tell me they don't have time to read, I always think of my mother, who put herself through nursing school while working full-time as a hairdresser with two kids under the age of eight. She loves to read, but she didn't have time to read a full book at that juncture in her life. So she read magazines, usually just an article or two before going to bed at 1 a.m. and then doing it all over again. If she can do it, you can do it.

Set a timer. If you're not used to reading, ten minutes is going to feel exceptionally long. If your mind wanders off the page and you keep checking the timer to see how much time is left, it's fine. Just keep on reading for the full ten minutes. Give your brain time to settle down. In terms of when to read, that's up to you, but I'll recommend the following: any scenario where you're waiting in a certain place (waiting in line, waiting for an appointment), first thing in the morning before the demands of the day begin, right before bed to wind down, on your lunch break from work. Find a pocket of time.

SWAP ONE ACTIVITY YOU NORMALLY DO WITH READING

A few years ago I had the honor of interviewing author Elizabeth Gilbert for an article on creativity. She told me a story about how once she was complaining to a friend about not having any time to write. Gilbert had all these reasons, and after she laid them out like playing cards, her friend said, "What are you willing to give up to have the life you say you want?" Mic drop.

Of course, using the "What are you willing to give up?" question for something like reading might seem dramatic, but the logic is the same. If you love to watch movies on the weekends, but you also want to read more frequently, then are you willing to give up one weekly movie-watching period to read instead? If the answer is no, I'll challenge you further: if you watch one movie per week, that's four movies a month. On the conservative side, that's probably six hours of screen time—and you're telling me you can't, in a single month, devote a measly quarter of that time to a book? Or maybe you're die-hard about your daily workouts. For one week, what would happen if you skipped your morning run or evening high-intensity interval session and instead gave yourself a mental pass to read? None of this is mandatory, but what are you willing to give up to do the thing you say you want to do?

TRY THIS

Think of how you spend your time, and pick one short window in which you could read something. If you're not sure where to start, just pay attention to your choices throughout a regular day, and ask yourself if you could swap out what you're doing with reading. Then replace that activity with a few pages of a book, flip through a magazine or newspaper, or finally dive into an article. Better yet, combine the two, such as reading while you're on public transportation or in the bathtub or on the treadmill. Don't think of your reading time as something to be completed, either—you certainly don't have to finish an entire chapter, read from cover to cover, or scroll to the end.

SET A MONTHLY READING GOAL

My own personal goal is to read two books a month as well as read something printed (i.e., not on a screen) for at least fifteen minutes a day, three days a week. Do I reach that goal every month? Nooooo. But without it I end up reading exactly zero books and spend too much time snuggled up with my laptop, so that's why I keep a target in mind. Yours doesn't have to be that specific, either—you can focus more on the amount of time and frequency (like a half hour every week at the minimum) or a certain style (at least one nonfiction book per month), or you can aim toward quantity (one book in general, no matter the topic). This will help you stay accountable and actually follow through.

And be realistic. You're not on vacation swaying in a hammock with a drink in hand (although that is a very lovely way to read!)—you're living your real life, which is likely full of people, things, work, and events. Don't come down hard on yourself for missing a couple of months in a row, and if you feel like overachieving, that's great. My best advice is to take what seems realistic and push a little bit further. If you were able to find ten minutes in the easy challenge to read, see if you can do that a few times a week for an entire month or every day for a month, or even extend that time to twenty minutes. If you enjoyed carving out a certain amount of time per week to read rather than a different activity you normally do, then strive for that every week for a month. Or make your goal about the reading material itself: "I will read a section of the paper every morning."

Be Intentional with Screen Time

You've likely heard the panic over what screen time is doing to our brains and bodies, and I'm not here to stoke the fire. However, I think it's clear, especially if you're over the age of twenty or so, that screens and devices rule our lives, which makes technology addictive.

I grew up in the nineties and early aughts. TV, computers, and smartphones all existed, but they were tangible, separate items used for specific purposes. I remember watching *Sabrina, the Teenage Witch* on Friday nights with my sisters, eating pizza, and talking about our crushes. Movies were saved for special occasions at the theater or a weekend treat via Blockbuster rental. Our main phone sat in the kitchen attached to a cord, and we had a real-life answering machine. Cell phones were for emergencies, and when I got one at age sixteen, I had a limited amount of minutes until 9 p.m. and texting required T9 words.

Times have obviously changed. Now, if you want boundaries related to screen time, you have to implement them yourself—which is both smart and seemingly impossible.

TAKE A BREAK FROM ONE TYPE OF SCREEN FOR PART OF YOUR DAY

There's an age-old dieting "rule" that suggests picking between a cocktail, the bread basket, and dessert at each meal, instead of enjoying all three. I don't subscribe to this—I mean, sometimes a person needs a glass of pinot noir, a breadstick, *and* the chocolate pudding—but I think the logic is helpful in terms of how you approach screen time.

Most days, at least in my life, I'm utilizing every screen available: I'm on my computer and glancing at my phone with the TV on in the background. This not only makes me feel distracted and scatterbrained but is also kind of...unnecessary? Like, can't I just enjoy one at a time?

Apparently not, unless I'm mindful about doing so. That's why taking a break from at least one type of screen is nice in a given day. Maybe you put your phone on airplane mode or leave it in the other room plugged in or on the charger. Maybe you decide not to watch any TV that night. Maybe you skip the extra laptop time after being on a computer for work purposes all day long. Then notice what it feels like to be without it. For me, it's a little weird at the beginning; I feel like I'm missing something or I forgot to do something. I'll even reach for my phone automatically, like a phantom limb, before realizing it's not accessible. Which is exactly why this exercise is such a helpful way to reset.

It doesn't matter how long your break lasts, though I recommend at least fifteen to thirty minutes. Just practice being intentional with how you use your technology, and see what it feels like to eliminate one option for a short period of time.

UNPLUG FOR AN ENTIRE DAY

Before you freak out, remember that it's just one day of your life. It's going to be hard. It's gonna feel odd and then kind of refreshing and then absolutely delightful. You'll likely go through that entire pattern of emotions, even if you try this exercise more than once, so be prepared. Also, keep it simple. You don't need to spend five thousand hours to fly to a remote spa where there's no Wi-Fi or modern electricity. Just put your devices in a basket or another room, leave them alone, and shut off the devices around you for twenty-four hours. (Yes, checking *Facebook* counts.)

Think back to a couple of decades ago. All sorts of regular activities— driving the car, listening to music, pondering a question, exercising—were things people just did. I don't mean to sound like a Luddite longing for the good old days. I definitely argued with my mom every night for permission to dial up my AOL Instant Messenger. But I also spent a lot of time hanging out with my sisters, racing around our backyard, going to gymnastics, practicing piano, and sitting on the kitchen counter.

Technology has incredible power to connect and inform and streamline, which is amazing. But technology can also become addictive, too, and it's worth taking a full day once in a while to unplug to realize that fact.

TRY THIS

If the idea of unplugging for a full day freaks you out, start with unplugging during a specific event. Enjoy a cup of coffee without mindlessly browsing on your phone. Eat dinner with a friend and actually focus on him the entire time instead of updating your status. Go outside instead of opening your computer, or skip automatically turning on the TV the second you get home. An easy question to ask yourself is this: "Do I need my phone/computer/TV right now?" If the answer is no, do something else. Over time those little moments of unplugging will add up, and you'll recognize when you turn to a screen out of a habit versus when you're making a deliberate choice.

TRACK YOUR SCREEN TIME AND MAKE A PLAN TO REDUCE IT

If you've completed the medium-level challenge, then you know the feeling of freedom that can accompany being screen-free for a period of time. The goal here is to give yourself that feeling more often by tracking and then reducing the amount of time you spend on screens. If you immediately think, *Well, I'm not on my phone that much,* think again—I read recently that the average American spends upward of four to five hours *a day* consuming media through a screen.

That five minutes you spend before making your breakfast in the morning, those twenty minutes curled up on the couch scrolling through your *Instagram* feed, that TV show you start watching because your spouse left the TV on...all those chunks of time probably don't even register in your brain until you actually stop and notice them.

Then once you have a realistic picture of how often you are actually on a screen, make a goal for how much time to eliminate. And I'm not talking about eliminating it just today. I mean eliminate it *forever*. You may need to come up with a rule to get yourself into the habit at first. For example, some people will allow themselves to check social media only if they are standing. That way they are more likely to spend less time doing it because standing or pacing in your kitchen is not as comfortable as curling up on a couch or lying in your bed looking through your feed. One trick that works for me? I put my phone out of sight during periods of the day when I know I shouldn't be on it. Instead of leaving it on my desk at work, I'll place it in my bag; in the mornings and evenings at home, I plug it into the charger upstairs instead of bringing it with me room to room.

Then keep track of your usage every day and see if you can improve upon your previous week's time.

CHALLENGE #9:
Have Fun

I'm a type A high performer. I like my life to feel full, with multiple plates spinning in the air and a dozen different options at my fingertips. I also like to get things done, check the box, do it right, excel. Most of the activities and endeavors I pursue have a specific purpose with clearly marked touchpoints along the way, and plenty of time for reflection and review at the end.

I approached yoga teacher training in the same way. I wanted to learn as much as possible. I wanted to be "good" at teaching yoga. I studied the poses, learned about anatomy, tried to sequence my classes to perfection, and picked out ideal compilations of songs for my students. I meant well. I also forgot that it was supposed to be fun. On the last day of our training, we sat in a giant circle and one of the teachers guiding our group passed around a bucket of small rocks, each with a word written on it. Everyone pulled a rock out of the bucket, and that word "spoke" to you for a certain reason, or not, all in good fun. My turn came and I pulled out a stone, assuming I'd select a very insightful, deep, thoughtful word, like *courage* or *purpose* or *devotion*. Instead, I got *play*.

I burst out laughing. The universe had had enough of my serious mindset; it wanted to remind me to have *fun* once in a while. I still have that rock, too, as a reminder to lighten up. Life is plenty serious already. Invite some joy in.

DO SOMETHING THAT MAKES YOU RIDICULOUSLY HAPPY

What's something that makes you feel lighthearted, cheerful, and upbeat—for no reason at all? And when's the last time you let yourself feel that way? What comes to mind for me: dancing to music in the kitchen, sitting outside on my back deck with a cold beverage, watching hokey teen dramas, baking cookies, coloring, arranging flowers, writing down quotes and song lyrics, walking through farmers' markets, riding a bike, exploring libraries or bookstores, texting GIFs back and forth with my sister, checking out a coffee shop in a new city, and so on. None of these things necessarily serve a purpose. I don't get graded or paid or even told "good job." But in the grand scheme of life, these simple pleasures are bright spotlights against the humdrum of daily existence.

Think of one thing you can do today that's purely for fun, and then give yourself permission to do it, no strings attached. How does it make you feel? Can you let yourself cut loose for a happiness boost, just for a moment? Pick something that brings you joy, regardless of whether it makes sense to anyone else.

GIVE YOURSELF PERMISSION TO NOT BE PRODUCTIVE

There are all sorts of life hacks intended to help you use your time in a way that generates output. Productivity makes us feel good, like we're moving the ball forward and having an impact. But sometimes making a decision or taking an action doesn't need to be "productive." We're accustomed to categorizing our choices as entirely productive (valuable and results-oriented) or pointless (frivolous and unnecessary due to lack of results). This is a false juxtaposition, especially when it comes to your own sense of play, fun, and happiness. Plenty of choices exist in the latter category that are worth doing and exploring, and in the same breath, you can do a hell of a lot of productive things that aren't very "meaningful" at all.

Think about what you liked to do as a kid—or if you're around kids, think about what *they* might do in terms of playing and having fun in a "non-adult" way. It can be planned or totally spontaneous. I'll give you an example. Most weeks my husband and I get home and immediately launch into productive activities: a load of dishes, wiping down counters, throwing laundry in the dryer, prepping dinner. But one day my husband opened a FedEx box that included a ton of bubble wrap. Messy, noisy, distracting. Instead of throwing it away—you know, the responsible, productive thing to do—he laid all of it out on the floor to make a path for our two-year-old to run and stomp all over it. And you know what? We had a blast.

TRY THIS

Pick an evening where you have nothing going on: no plans, no commitments, no truly serious obligations to take into consideration. Then refrain from doing anything productive, like household chores or meal prep or catching up on work emails. You're probably going to feel guilty, like you're "wasting" time—which you are. That's the whole point. You can afford to spend a couple hours as a human *being*, not a human *doing*. For every impulse to do something or shift into worker bee status, tell yourself, "My only job is to be myself tonight." That's it.

START A HOBBY OR ACTIVITY THAT'S PURELY FOR YOUR OWN ENJOYMENT

My friend Jami likes to paint on top of old *New York Times* newspapers and then make little collages. My husband decided last year to start a garden on a whim, which he filled with fruits and vegetables, just to see what might grow and what wouldn't in our backyard. My sister-in-law, who happens to be excellent at sourcing cool clothes from thrift stores, asked for a sewing machine at Christmas so she could learn how to make her own clothing. My mom likes to buy little gifts and knickknacks for people when she's out and about, so when they need a pick-me-up, she has something on hand to send over right away. My dad meets a group of retired fellow police officers every morning to drink cheap coffee and shoot the bull over *The Andy Griffith Show*. Me? I like to soak in the tub a few nights a week with overpriced bubble bath and a magazine.

Too often people think about hobbies and immediately stress about the amount of time, money, or energy involved to get started. But the truth is that a hobby can be anything. It doesn't have to be productive or make sense. You can explore one at any age, whenever you feel like it. At its core, it's just an activity that makes you happy. It's fun. And that's why it's worth doing.

So what would you love to do, simply for your own enjoyment, if you had all the time and money in the world? What are you curious about? It doesn't have to be related to your career, match what people expect of you, or even be something you liked five years ago. Pick one or two things that come to mind, and give them a try. If you've always wanted to learn a second language, get a book from the library and make flash cards. If you wish you were a better cook, find a recipe you'd love to master, purchase the ingredients, and give it a go. If you always wanted to knit a scarf, look up some *YouTube* videos and head to a fabric store. Whatever sounds fun to you is worth exploring.

Make Peace with Who You're Not

I know, I know—normally you're told to take risks and get outside your comfort zone and live on the edge and find yourself. I, however, would like to argue on behalf of recognizing who you're *not*. Obviously this can and will change over the years, because all human beings can and will change. But there's a certain freedom that comes with understanding yourself, your likes and dislikes, and owning those facts. For example, I consider myself an introvert, and I spent years feeling sorta bad about it—as though I should try to be more outgoing and talkative and gregarious. Even when I did try to amp up parts of my personality to fit that mold, I mostly felt weird and fake. Finally, I decided to accept the fact that I would always veer to the side of introspective and quiet, which actually now serves as one of my top strengths.

MAKE A LIST OF WHAT YOU DON'T LIKE

Chances are you probably know exactly what you don't like—and either you're the type of person who shouts it to the world, because you're set in your ways and unwilling to be flexible, or you keep it to yourself, because you don't want to offend anyone and end up being overly flexible. There's a big difference, though, between handing out loud opinions like candy and articulating what truly doesn't work for you in a respectful way. One very real element of knowing what you don't like involves recognizing that other people like those exact same things, and that's more than acceptable. For instance, I've learned that I'm not a fan of soda, crowded parties, most sporting events, dancing at clubs, and sauerkraut. Every time I try to be open-minded about one of these things, I soon realize, *Yeah, no, this isn't for me.* As Amy Poehler says in her book, *Yes Please*, "Good for her! Not for me."

Take a couple of minutes to write down things you just don't really care for, without trying to convince yourself to like them or try them again *and* without thinking about what anyone else would say about it.

STOP DOING THAT ONE THING YOU SECRETLY HATE

It's strange how we often say yes to things to make other people happy, and even stranger that we tend to do it repeatedly, even after all evidence has proven we don't like the thing we've agreed to do. While venturing outside of your norm, especially on behalf of or with someone you care about, can be a fantastic adventure, I'm talking about situations where you literally *know* you don't want to go to the meeting, join the committee, meet for coffee—and yet you still do it. Dude, stop! Just stop.

This week look at your calendar and take inventory of all the things you would not choose. Some will need to be done anyway, like paying bills or showing up to work on time. But I'm willing to bet that at least one thing falls in the category of "I said yes, but I hate this, ugh, why?" Like networking, or a random proposal for a project that you have little interest in, or Snapchat. Instead of doing that crappy task, just say no.

TRY THIS

Look at all of your plans for the next month or two. If there's anything on your calendar that instantly makes you feel annoyed or seems like a giant "should," cross it out. Cancel the plans. Say no. Then take a second to reflect: is [fill in the blank] actually important to you or not? Some of our "shoulds" serve a deeper purpose, like exercising or volunteering, where you need to push past that initial discomfort for the right reasons. Other times it's a self-inflicted obligation based on who we think we ought to be, rooted in our ego. One way to figure out the difference: tell a friend all the reasons why the activity at hand is valuable to you specifically, and ask your friend to tally the number of times you use phrases like "have to" or "want to" or "should." Generally speaking, you'll probably notice a pattern that'll indicate how you really feel about the plans in question.

OWN WHAT YOU DON'T LIKE AND DON'T FEEL SHAMED FOR IT

In college I went to a lot of parties—mostly because my friends did, and that's what I thought you were supposed to do in college, even though I didn't *like* parties very much. The vast majority of the time, they were too loud with too many people and cheap drinks; I couldn't have a full conversation with anyone or find a place to sit down, all of which completely wore out my introverted tendencies.

And the dancing. Oh, the dancing. Despite twelve years of ballet under my belt as a kid, dancing at a party (or even worse, at a club) was the opposite of fun to me. I hated it. I wanted to sit in a dim bar with comfortable booths and a delicious craft beer and talk to my friends or new people in a chill vibe. Instead I found myself in a lot of situations where I was at a party where everyone danced, and I felt angst over wanting to seem fun and cool and game, but also knowing the scene just wasn't *me*. Once I remember standing at a house party with my then-boyfriend, red Solo cup in my hand, trying to fit in. One of his pals came up to me and asked why I wasn't dancing. "Oh, I don't know; I don't really want to," I replied. "Come on, at least *try* to be fun," he teased curtly. *Ouch.* I weakly smiled—mostly because at nineteen years old, I didn't feel confident enough to call him an asshole, nor did I realize I could *not* like things other people liked without shame or a sense of insecurity. I also felt like if I responded to him, I'd have to launch into a long story about why I didn't like parties, which seemed exhausting even then.

Now I know better. And I'll tell you the same thing: you can own what you don't like without constantly feeling like you have to explain or defend how you feel. That's how we live by our values and priorities, and it's a good skill to cultivate.

Part 2

Health

If a silver bullet solution existed for health, then I wouldn't be writing this section—and the entire healthcare industry would cease to exist, along with the millions of books and articles and experts out there, because everyone would be, well, healthy. Of course, the reality is that human beings get sick and injured all the time, and while medicine and technology have improved vastly in the past few centuries, people will still continue to get sick to some degree. You can approach everything "right" in terms of health and still run into health challenges. Which may seem fatalistic—I mean, nobody lives forever, so you might as well eat buckets of French fries, smoke a pack a day, stay up late every night, and never move your body, right? Well, maybe not.

However, I do believe health is wealth, and there are certain basic activities or strategies that best serve nearly everyone in the long run. In this part you'll learn about practicing yoga and meditation, finding time to work out, eating less sugar and drinking more water, getting enough sleep, and meal planning. We'll also talk about the importance of knowing your health history, appreciating your body, and defining what self-care looks like for *you*.

CHALLENGE #1:
Practice Yoga

I started practicing yoga around 2010 as an overwhelmed graduate student working full-time in Chicago. At the time I felt lost, unsure, and alone, and that one hour of stretching and breathing reminded me of my own strength and presence. Eventually I got my two-hundred-hour certification and taught yoga for several years. The number one question I was asked in that time was this: "How do I start practicing yoga?"

Which tends to make me laugh. Not because I can't empathize—I totally appreciate the genuine desire to explore yoga, and I definitely can relate to not knowing exactly how or when to begin. But at the risk of sounding like every other yoga teacher I've ever met, I'm sorry to say there's no mysterious answer. In fact, it's pretty straightforward: you just start. Today. Before you buy a cute yoga outfit, before you find the best studio in town, before you research unfamiliar terms, before you master a single pose, before you're skinny enough or fit enough or "good" enough... before any of that, you can start a yoga practice.

DO FIVE MINUTES OF YOGA

People sometimes assume yoga is saying "ommmm" in a circle holding hands, but it's much broader and more customizable than you think. The word *yoga* means "to yoke," or "to unite"; it's a chance to unite breath and movement to feel a sense of union within yourself. How that takes shape for you will vary. But on a single day, you can try on this accessible yoga practice for size.

1. Set a timer for one to five minutes. Stand or sit in a quiet spot, and bring your hands together at the center of your chest, near your heart, with palms pressed together and elbows flaring out wide. Feel your thumbs connect to your breastbone.
2. Lift the top of your head up tall and soften your shoulders. Draw your belly in on a slow inhale, then exhale as you allow your belly to expand. Breathe like this until the timer goes off.

At first, it'll probably feel ridiculously easy or even boring. Stay with it. Pay attention to what comes up physically, emotionally, and mentally. Try not to judge; just let it all roll. Whenever I do this little practice, my mind starts chattering: *My nose itches. I don't wanna do this. I wonder how tomorrow's meeting will go. Did I send that email? I need to call my grandma. Has it been a minute yet? This is the longest minute ever. I wish I were better at this...*

Usually, my distracted mind quiets down, and I can focus on just breathing. When the timer goes off, you're done. You did yoga.

TRY THIS

Do a body scan. Close your eyes, and with a steady breath, think about relaxing every part of your body. Start with your feet: uncurl your toes, wiggle them around, and stretch your arches. Move your mind through your lower half and upper body, all the way to the crown of your head. When you're done, blink your eyes open and take another round of breath. You can use this body scan to reset anytime you feel overwhelmed.

TRY FIVE BEGINNER YOGA POSES

Did you know there are eight limbs of yoga and physical postures are just one of them? Most people assume handstands or pretzel poses on a beach equal yoga—but traditionally yoga includes disciplines such as *pranayama* (breathing), *niyama* (positive duties), *yama* (moral disciplines), and *dharana* (focused concentration), among others. Bodily movement, known as *asana*, is just one option.

In a given week, you can certainly focus on the physical, as it's often the easiest place to start. But for this challenge, focus on what you can learn in a few short days. Find a resource that provides a little bit of information: a friend who is obsessed with yoga and willing to show you some basic poses, a *YouTube* breakdown, a library book that outlines introductory postures, or even a local class at a studio or gym. Try to learn something new each day of this week. Notice I did not say, "Learn these poses and perfect them in order to receive your first-place medal in yoga performance." Let's agree to take it easy on ourselves, yeah?

Match your body to what some of these poses look like, and try to hold each pose for three to five breaths. If you do something on one leg, like a Warrior II lunge, then do it on the other side too. You might wonder what the hell you're doing; your muscles may shake. All of this is normal. At the root of yoga is curiosity, and with this challenge, like the daylong one, your job is to try some of these poses and experience what they're like. (Disclaimer: always talk to your doctor before doing yoga or beginning any type of exercise routine.)

COMPLETE FOUR YOGA CLASSES

The biggest mistake most people make when starting a yoga practice is attempting too much, too soon. I admire the desire to dedicate yourself to a daily yoga practice, but when you're starting from scratch, doing something every single day is exhausting. It's easy to fail when you overload your brain and your body with a new initiative, so if you want to do a monthlong yoga challenge, I invite you to start with a weekly practice.

The task? Complete four yoga classes, one per week. Length and style of class doesn't matter much—you can do the exact same online class four times, go to four different instructors at your gym, or switch between a fifteen-minute vinyasa flow at home and a seventy-five-minute restorative class at a studio. Just find four and put them on your calendar. If cost is an issue, look for free options through community clubs or resources or web-based platforms, which usually offer a free first class or an introductory week at minimum.

If you start slow, then I have no doubt you can work up to a daily yoga practice. In the meantime, stay patient and humble; you'll likely be tempted to skip at least one of these four sessions once you get going. I can say all of this with love, mostly because I've been there before. Keep it simple and don't overthink it.

CHALLENGE #2:
Meditate

Ten years ago, if I heard the word *meditation*, I imagined sitting cross-legged on a braided rug for a long stretch of time with my eyes closed and weird humming noises coming out of my mouth. I equated such behavior with hippies, or really serious yogis, or at least people with long hair and an affinity for New Age magic. I also didn't think the benefits exceeded past a little stress relief and probably a related sense of self-improvement. But as I stumbled across articles and studies on meditation, and went through my own yoga teacher training, my skepticism slowly morphed into something like curiosity.

Now I realize meditation is more than smoke and mirrors—the health benefits alone are backed by legitimate research, and plenty of it. Meditation can lower stress and anxiety, reduce your risk of heart disease and depression, improve your self-esteem, foster better coping mechanisms, help with weight management, and complement exercise performance. And at the *very* least, it allows our busy brains to take a little break from always thinking, striving, planning, and analyzing. Maybe you're still not convinced, and that's fine, but it can't hurt to give it a try, either.

TAKE FIVE INTENTIONAL BREATHS

Breathing exercises seem sort of silly at first. I mean, we all breathe; otherwise we wouldn't be alive. Why does it need to be practiced or observed or explored? Because most of the time, many of us breathe shallow, short breaths, and that sort of inhale and exhale pattern doesn't do much more than keep your body functioning at a bare minimum. When you play around with different breath patterns, you can feel how your body adapts and reacts; you can learn to control your breath, slow it down or speed it up, and use it as a tool to counteract feelings of fight-or-flight —all of which proves plenty helpful in busy lives, relationships, and health-related matters.

I first tried counting intentional breaths in a yoga class, though I was familiar with the general concept around taking deep breaths amid stressful moments. It's essentially the same concept: you count to one on your inhale, then count to one on your exhale. You count to two on your inhale, then count to two on your exhale. Work your way up to the count of five, and most importantly, go as slow as possible. Allow your breath to make noise; you can even place your hands on your belly to feel it rise and fall, or close your eyes to avoid distraction. Use this exercise at any moment, in any location, for any situation where you feel overwhelmed or like you need to pause or hit the reset button. And almost every time, you'll probably discover that you feel a little more in control, a little calmer, as a result. Breathing for five seconds doesn't eliminate life problems, but it does give your mind a chance to back off from a negative thought pattern or stop freaking out about something, and in a physical sense, it sends oxygen to your parasympathetic nervous system to reduce the amount of cortisol in your blood, which minimizes stress and panic.

DO INTENTIONAL BREATHING TWO TO FIVE MINUTES EVERY DAY FOR A WEEK

As an effective strategy with nearly immediate benefits, the five-breath exercise is an easy one to keep in your back pocket for stressful situations. I use it all the time. But it's sort of like eating a salad once in a while after indulging in too many burgers on a regular basis; because you're employing it as an immediate change or a way to regroup, the impact on how you feel is pretty apparent. Taking meditation up a level, then, involves doing it more regularly in small increments and building from there, which is where a lot of people get stuck based on the assumption that it's not "doing" anything.

For this challenge, start by deciding what type of intentional breathing works for you. I like the count method because it gives me something to focus on, but there are plenty of other types, such as alternate-nostril breathing, mantra or visualization tactics, or inhale-exhale breathing for a set period of time. You can try all of these until you land on one that seems to resonate or feels more approachable, and then set a timer for every day of a week to practice that breathing. If you're brand-new to meditation, I recommend starting with two minutes each day, and if you've experimented with meditating before, anywhere between two and five minutes total is fine. Don't feel compelled to over-achieve here and try to meditate for twenty minutes a day—and I don't say that to be discouraging, only to emphasize that I've done that exact thing before and failed, and I've seen other people make the same mistake. Worry less about the amount of time, and focus on consistency. If you can do it around the same time of day, great, but if you can't, don't sweat it.

COMMIT TO SIXTY-SIX DAYS OF MEDITATION

It takes about two months (hence the sixty-six days!) to turn a behavior into a sustainable habit. Along with consistency, habits also require motivation throughout a cycle of cues, cravings, responses, and rewards.

So how do you motivate yourself to meditate? Using a meditation app or calendar can keep you accountable while forming a good habit. These tools remove the legwork, offer structure, and encourage you to keep going through completion goals and reward techniques (which promote good habits). This approach also exposes you to all the different types of meditation styles that exist, such as ones with a speaking voice, mantras, music, or even a tailored series for sleeping or energy. You can go the old-school route, set a timer for five minutes, and use the intentional breathing strategy from the previous challenges. Or you can try a longer meditation—lots of people love fifteen-, twenty-, or even thirty-minute exercises. Find a meditation style and length that you can actually do for two months, every single day.

TRY THIS

For the next sixty-six days, do a two-minute mantra meditation each morning. Here's how it works: after you wake up, but before you get ready or reach for your coffee, sit in a quiet space and close your eyes. Use the mantra "I am enough" as a phrase to focus on. With every inhale, think *I am*. On the exhale, think the word *enough*. Repeat with each breath for two minutes. You can swap out this mantra for another short saying, or extend the length of time at any point—just be sure to complete the meditation in the same spot, in roughly the same way, every day for the two-month period.

CHALLENGE #3:
Find Time to Work Out

The number one excuse I hear friends, family, and acquaintances use with respect to not working out involves lack of time. (Or that exercising is too hard, which...it's supposed to be. If it were easier, more people would do it without any resistance.) I've gotten to the point now where I don't even bother hiding my eye roll in response to the whole "I don't have time" reasoning—mainly because I firmly believe you have time for whatever is important to you. If you "don't have time," it's not generally because you straight up don't have the time in your schedule; it's because the thing in question is not important to you, and you're not interested in prioritizing your schedule to make time for it. Which, let me be clear, is okay! There are plenty of seasons in life where certain things take a back seat, or you change as a person and what used to be important to you isn't anymore, or you're dealing with a bigger issue and don't have the mental or emotional or physical capacity to take on one more thing.

Exercise boosts endorphins, protects your heart, strengthens your bones and muscles, lowers stress, and makes you feel like a better version of yourself. It's worth doing and it's good for you, so if you want to exercise and you are healthy and able-bodied, then you likely have time. Some of the busiest people I know find a way to work out regularly for their health, and they're willing to sacrifice something to make it happen. For them, exercise is a nonnegotiable because of how it makes them feel. In this challenge I'll explain why short walks are the gateway to a regular routine, and how a little exploration can help you figure out your soulmate workout.

GO FOR A SHORT WALK

In my opinion, walking is one of the very best forms of exercise: it's free, fairly accessible to most ages and body types, and available almost anywhere, and you don't need special clothes or shoes or gear. In a world of hot vinyasa yoga, marathons, heavy weights, burpees, and protein shakes, walking offers a low-impact way to stay active. Walking is also really good for your body—it can prevent conditions like heart disease, high blood pressure, and type 2 diabetes, and it helps with weight loss, builds muscle and endurance, supports coordination and balance, and improves your mood.

You can also take a walk in under fifteen minutes, which is what I do when I'm super busy but want to find at least one tiny window for physical activity. I know, I know, you're probably saying, "Fine, but a walk isn't the same thing as a *workout*." That's where I beg to differ, even though I understand where you're coming from. I, too, used to think a true workout meant at least an hour of movement, buckets of sweat dripping down my face, specialty movement requiring a teacher's direction, loud music, and a very sore body the next day. False. Exercise can certainly mean any of those things, but it can also mean taking your dog for a ten-minute stroll around the block, just enough to get your heart rate pumping slightly. Walking is nice and an excellent way to keep your body moving if you're short on time.

TRY THREE TYPES OF WORKOUTS

I know so many folks who claim they don't have time to work out simply because they've decided in advance that it'll be terrible, myself included. Two pieces of advice: first, try to let go of any preconceived notions of what you think exercise will be like, based on either previous experience or some other notion in your head. Second, allow yourself to wonder what it would be like to enjoy exercise. I mean, what if exercise was...fun? Can you even imagine?

From this clean mental slate, in the course of a week, pick three types of workouts to try. Maybe you've done them before, maybe you haven't; it doesn't matter. Be open-minded with variety and length, get creative, ask around, and don't spend a bunch of time or money trying to perfectly plan out the best three forms of exercise you could possibly do. Then, see what you like and what you don't. Maybe the whole going-to-a-class thing was not your jam, and you realized you despise biking indoors. Maybe you preferred to combine friend time and a hilly stroll. Maybe you appreciated being able to do a workout from social media in your living room. Maybe you tried all of these things and then thought, *Nah, I'll stick to running.* But over the course of a week, try on a few workout styles for size and evaluate which ones you'd potentially do again.

TRY THIS

Most gyms and studios offer perks to first-timers, like free or reduced-rate passes and classes, so use those benefits to your advantage in terms of investigating new workout options. Find three places where you can exercise or take a fitness class with little or no financial investment. (If you're not sure what's available, look up locations online, as that information is usually on a website somewhere, or call and ask!) Challenge yourself to pick options outside of your comfort zone, and then give each one a go within the same week. At the end of the week, treat yourself to something health-related that feels special, like a green juice or workout attire.

DO THE WORKOUT YOU LIKE THE MOST AT LEAST TWICE A WEEK

Building on the momentum of the previous challenge, take the workout you liked the most (or hated the least!) and plan to do it at least twice a week. For example, if you discovered that you loved the buddy system for accountability purposes, and joining a friend for a walk or run seemed to be the easiest way to follow through on working out regularly, then use that same model in a given month but amp up the frequency. Ask your friend if you can get together on Tuesdays and Thursdays at 7 a.m. for a thirty-minute workout, before you both head to the office.

Actively choosing a form of exercise you don't hate is the first step in creating a habit of working out. And you're essentially committing to doing it eight times in the span of a month, which doesn't feel impossible. You retain your autonomy—you get to choose what form of movement you do this month—and you set the terms, because the length of workout doesn't matter, either. It can be ten minutes or one hour, on your own or in the mode of a formal class. Your job is to move twice a week.

CHALLENGE #4:
Eat Less Sugar

I've spent six years in healthcare communications and devoted much of that time to content and executive marketing strategies. One thing I've learned: when it comes to health, consumers know what is and isn't good for them, and with respect to the latter, sometimes they don't care. Seriously. I can preach about the perils of processed meat all day long, for instance, but if you think bacon is delicious and traditionally fry up a pan of it for Sunday morning brunch with your family every week, the health benefits (or lack thereof) don't actually matter much. The same is true for sugar. You already know a giant cinnamon roll isn't good for your health. But you're going to eat one once in a while, health knowledge be damned. Still, moderation is key, and on the topic of added, nonnatural sugar specifically, we'd all probably do well with slightly backing off. Here's how.

CUT OR ELIMINATE THE EXTRA SUGAR IN ONE FOOD OR BEVERAGE

Unfortunately you can find sugar in almost *everything*, and what makes matters more complicated is the fact that sugar comes in different forms. Some experts claim fruit has too much sugar and you should avoid it, while others warn against only the grams of sugar found in overly processed items like juice or dessert, and that's not even including all the so-called sugar-free options out there. It gets confusing, fast. That's why a good place to start involves looking at a normal day of your eats, and simply noticing where you could cut or eliminate added, unnecessary sugar. Perhaps you habitually add sugar of some form to your daily coffee—if so, for a day you could drink your coffee with half as much of that sugar, or none at all. Perhaps you typically enjoy a square of dark chocolate or a cookie after dinner every night, and tonight you'll pass.

You don't have to fall on the sword of "Sugar is the devil, and I'm not allowed to ever have it again." You're just practicing the behavior of making an active choice: every time you eat or drink something, you can decide to try to reduce the amount of sugar involved. You don't have to be perfect at this. I'll go out on a limb and say that in my opinion, sugar in moderation is a normal part of life, mostly because I like donuts but also because I don't think an all-or-nothing mentality works well. But I do notice that when I try to make those minor daily adjustments to my sugar intake, it's easier to consume less sugar overall.

CUT OR ELIMINATE THE SUGAR IN ONE FOOD OR BEVERAGE FOR EVERY MEAL

Take the same process you used in the previous challenge and apply it to every single beverage or meal in a given week. You don't have to say no to the sugar; just begin to notice how much sugar is already potentially in your diet, and ask yourself: "Do I want or need this?" I'm not a nutritionist or a dietitian, so I'm certainly not outlining a diet plan for you or even offering a professional opinion on the merits or drawbacks of quantities of sugar in your eating routine. But as a regular person who has tried hard to cool it on sugar once in a while, this works well for me, especially in the framework of a week. I almost immediately notice where I'm mindlessly adding or eating sugary items versus making an intentional choice.

Some trade-offs I've made as a result: skipping the grocery store cookies in favor of my aunt's homemade chocolate chip. Both obviously have sugar, but one feels like a special treat worthy of the indulgence, and the other? I could honestly do without it and not feel deprived. Or the realization that I like a little brown sugar in my iced coffee, so I add half a teaspoon instead of the three I used to dump in. All those tiny changes add up to less sugar consumed overall, while I can still enjoy sugar in moderation.

KEEP A FOOD JOURNAL OF HOW MUCH SUGAR YOU CONSUME

You might already be familiar with food journaling, and it's one of those things people either love or hate—mostly because once you write down what you're eating, it's harder to argue against what you see on paper. You might *think* you're eating five servings of vegetables per day, only to realize you're barely making it to two. And when it comes to sugar, again, it sneaks into everything from dessert to chips to salad dressings to condiments to alcohol, so actually tracking the amount of sugar you consume may be a little depressing at first.

It'll also be incredibly eye-opening. Whether you take a more scientific approach (measure every single gram of sugar you consume, no matter what) or you just generally track your meals and snacks and drinks (noting what probably has extra sugar and what doesn't), you'll at least get some insights into your habits and go-to sugar cravings. From there, you can make adjustments or find healthier alternatives. Feel free to use any form of food journal you like; I've found a simple piece of paper in a notebook or a Notes app on your phone or computer will do just fine.

TRY THIS

Keep a food log for seven days and track your added sugar intake. For processed, packaged, and canned foods, you may need to read ingredient labels to see exactly how much sugar is in an item. Things like fruits, vegetables, and grains will vary, so you can look those up online for sugar quantities. Pay attention to differences in your sugar intake while eating at home versus eating out. Do your best to eat as normally as possible throughout the seven days, then review your journal. How much sugar did you consume each day and throughout the entire exercise? Use that knowledge to cut your sugar intake by at least a third, and make adjustments going forward in terms of making healthier decisions.

\\\\|//

CHALLENGE #5:

Drink More Water

Staying hydrated is one of those life hacks that always strikes me as beyond boring—mostly because I get tired of drinking plain water, and I'm consequently not that great on making sure I drink enough! Also, the more water I drink, the more I have to use the bathroom, which gets annoying on the regular. But I admire coworkers and friends who carry around a huge water bottle all day long, and I *know* drinking water is good for me, so I've made a continual effort to quench my thirst with water first, fun beverage second. There's usually a ripple effect; the more water I drink, the more I notice when I'm not drinking enough water, and being dehydrated clearly results in fogginess, tiredness, lower energy levels, and a desire to snack, snack, snack because I'm actually just thirsty. Maybe you can relate. The good news? Drinking more water is in fact pretty easy to do with a couple of minor adjustments. Here's how.

DRINK AN EXTRA GLASS OF WATER

DIFFICULTY LEVEL:
EASY

Drinking enough water regulates fluid in the body, maintains your body temperature, and helps you digest food properly. It improves your memory, brain power, and even your workouts; it can help you lose weight and keep your blood pressure steady. And adding one extra glass of water to your usual routine serves as the easiest, most practical way to up your hydration levels. Don't obsess over hitting a certain number of ounces, or feel compelled to invest in a pretty container—although those mind tricks and incentives can later prove useful. Simply drink one extra glass of water. It might feel like a total chore, like taking your vitamins or cleaning the bathroom or being on a conference call, but grab a glass and fill 'er up. I like adding fresh fruit and herbs (favorite combo: lemon, cucumber, and mint) to a pitcher of water in the fridge to help me switch things up, and I also make myself drink a glass of water with every meal and snack to help stay on track. Considering the minimum recommendation is eight glasses of water per day, this just means nine total. (And if you're like, "Wow, eight glasses, huh?" don't worry; you can work up to that!)

You may not see a difference in the least, and that's okay. Pretend like you're watering plants and giving your body a little extra love to stay functioning.

SEE IF YOU CAN SWAP MOST OF YOUR BEVERAGES FOR WATER

When I notice I'm getting a little dehydrated (what's up, bright yellow pee?), the first thing I do is take a week to get back on track, and that usually involves cooling it on all drinks except water. That's right—no tea, coffee, milk, soda, juice, or alcohol. Just water. Rather than try to force myself to drink *more* water, I just trade out all my usual beverages for a glass of water. The result? I end up drinking more water throughout the week, and I tend to feel fuller and less tired after each meal. Sticking to water only is good for your bank account and your body; you cut down on artificial sweeteners and extra calories, and by skipping the vending machine or that evening glass of wine, you can save money too. I wouldn't say this exercise is the most enticing one in the world, but self-care and self-improvement sometimes mean doing the practical stuff. And it's kind of fun to just see if you are able to stick with it.

DRINK A GLASS OF WATER FIRST THING IN THE MORNING AND RIGHT BEFORE BED

This challenge tip comes straight from my little sister, who happens to be excellent at staying hydrated. She always bookends her days with a glass of water: first thing in the morning before doing anything else, and right before going to sleep. In true sisterly fashion, I started copying her, just to see if it would help me drink more water—and it did, almost shockingly so. I made it part of my routine for a month, like brushing my teeth, and after about four weeks, I really began to feel the difference. I felt thirstier, oddly enough, and I craved that hit of water to kick off or conclude my day. When I woke up and went straight to coffee at work, I hit a wall around 11 a.m. and found myself chugging water before lunch. And when I forgot my water glass downstairs, I ended up in the kitchen at 3 a.m., parched. The downside? Sometimes I had to really make myself drink the water because I wasn't in the mood, or I felt tired, or my stomach was already quite full.

Drinking water at these set times not only creates a positive habit but also keeps you hydrated overnight, promotes good digestion, improves your complexion, and reduces sugar and salt cravings—so say farewell to that late-night snack or oversized morning muffin, and bring on the clear skin and higher energy levels.

TRY THIS

For the next thirty days, use this ice-in-a-glass trick. Every night fill up a glass of water and drink it in the kitchen before you head to bed. Then take that same glass of water, fill it up with ice, and bring it to your bedroom. Put it on your side table or bathroom counter, whichever is more accessible, and carry on with your regular bedtime routine. In the morning, as soon as you wake up, drink the water from the melted ice. This way, you kick-start the hydration process each day.

Go to Bed On Time

I can still vividly remember the first couple of months after my son was born, when the level of pure exhaustion astounded me. I knew I would be tired, but I didn't quite understand exactly *how* tired—to the point of feeling nauseated, cranky, and overwhelmed. It seemed like I could never catch up on sleep, and anytime I did snag a few consecutive hours, I consequently felt like a brand-new person. Sleep had become a valuable asset, one I used to take for granted, and I finally understood how lack of sleep could be so incredibly detrimental to one's health and well-being. A good night's sleep gives your brain a much-needed rest, builds memory association and learning skills, fights infection, and repairs your muscles. Without solid sleep, you'll not only feel sleepy and less alert, but you'll also be more prone to eating unhealthy foods and struggling with fatigue.

Outside of sleep hygiene issues like sleep apnea, most people simply need to just go to bed earlier to make sure they're hitting the recommended number of hours per night. For adults, that's between eight and ten hours, but the exact amount varies depending on your needs. If you're constantly tired, here's how you can start going to bed on time to actually catch those z's.

GO TO BED FIFTEEN MINUTES EARLIER

I'm not a night owl, but give me a bowl of ice cream and a TV show, and I can easily stay up until midnight without really meaning to. It also takes me a while to wind down, which is tricky—either I'm not quite ready to do the bedtime dance, or I procrastinate and end up waiting much too long. The result? Lying in bed scrolling on my phone for an hour versus hurriedly brushing my teeth and trying to convince myself to wash my face. In my quest to have a more consistent bedtime, one that allowed me to get the amount of sleep I needed for the following day, I had to ease into it using fifteen-minute increments.

For example, I typically get ready for bed around 10 p.m. but don't end up *in* bed or asleep until close to 11 p.m. So I started getting ready at 9:45, which doesn't sound like much of a difference, but I ended up in bed by 10:15 or so, and fell asleep by 10:30, giving me a whole extra thirty minutes per night. Whatever your usual bedtime (and if you don't have one, this will help you establish at least a baseline), move it back by fifteen minutes one day.

IDENTIFY YOUR PRE-BEDTIME HABITS AND ADJUST THEM FOR BETTER SLEEP

When you think of your bedtime rituals, what comes to mind? You might assume you don't have any, but you probably do—habits like watching TV, drinking water, examining your face in the mirror, or looking at your phone. Some of these may make it harder for you to fall asleep; however, a few little tweaks can help bedtime go more smoothly.

For a long time, my evenings went like this: eat dinner, give my son a bath, read a couple of books together, head back downstairs for a movie with my husband and a glass of wine. Brush my teeth, wash my face, slap on some eye cream. Catch up on email in bed. Look at social media. Set my alarm, lament how late it was, and try to fall asleep. None of that was *wrong*, but I rarely felt rested, so I made some adjustments. I picked a couple of evenings to stay up later, but most nights I nixed TV after 9 p.m. I brushed my teeth and washed my face earlier, which encouraged a sense of relaxation and winding down. And the biggest change? I viewed my phone as off-limits once I physically got in bed. As a result I slept better overall, and I could fall asleep without needing to count a million sheep.

TRY THIS

Do a bedtime behavior audit. Write down your routine every night for a week and notice any patterns. Do you always watch TV before bed? Crave something sweet? Keep track of your actions and how they make you feel, then for the subsequent week, make specific swaps based on your ideal bedtime routine while tracking the results a second time. Maybe you love reading on your phone in bed, but you accidentally stay up until midnight three nights in a row—instead try reading a paperback book for a set amount of time, like fifteen minutes, before lights out. Identify what's interfering with a good night's sleep and adjust accordingly.

ESTABLISH A BEDTIME SWEET SPOT AND STICK TO IT

All you really need to cultivate in terms of getting enough sleep is what I like to call a bedtime "sweet spot": the window of time when you need to hit the hay in order to get the amount of sleep you need to wake up feeling refreshed. This bedtime can range wildly—for instance, my husband's sweet spot is between 10 and 11 p.m. If he goes to bed earlier than that, then he is wide awake at 3 or 4 a.m. Mine is more like 9 to 10 p.m.; if I go to bed on the earlier side, I wake up naturally around 6 a.m., and if I zonk out on the later side of that range, I can still wake up feeling good to leave on time for work. And regardless of whether it's 9 or 10 p.m., I can generally push myself to get up a little earlier without being completely worn-out, or I can enjoy sleeping in a bit. Going to bed before 9 p.m. or closer to 11 p.m.? No way. But staying in my own personal bedtime sweet spot? Perfect.

To figure out your sweet spot, you need more than a day or week. Give yourself a month to try out different bedtimes and see how each impacts you, for better or for worse. You're still aiming for the recommended six to eight hours of sleep a night, but you'll know you've found your exact sweet spot regarding an actual bedtime when it doesn't feel hard to fall asleep and you wake up (mostly) rested.

Pack Your Lunch

At my first couple of jobs out of college, I brought my lunch to work every day—primarily because I didn't have a lot of discretionary income, but also because that's how I grew up and what my parents modeled. Going out to eat (or in high school, buying the hot lunch for $1.25) was a luxury, saved for either special occasions or when we were out of sandwich bread at home. Spending $12 on a salad in downtown Chicago? Basically an hour's work, and definitely not worth it at the time. Even now, I've worked hard enough to be in a position where I could afford to buy my lunch more often, but I still prefer to pack it every day. I save money, I get to eat exactly what I want, I can use up leftovers, and I often end up making healthier choices too. Sound good to you? Here's how to start making your lunch at home, save money on a weekly basis, and find the right balance of eating out throughout a given month.

FIND A RECIPE THAT YOU COULD MAKE AT HOME AND PACK AS A LUNCH

Obviously everyone has a different threshold and budget for cooking, meal prep, and meal planning. Some people love to be, or need to be, as frugal as possible; others don't see the harm in high-quality ingredients for homemade dishes. Some hate leftovers, while other folks could eat the same turkey sandwich every day with no complaints, or maybe you're one of those people who prefer a bunch of snacks and little bites to get you through the day. The point is that you'll have to decide what fits your preferences, but on the whole—especially if you're newer to packing your lunch—you can start by picking out a recipe to prepare for the next day.

Ideally keep it simple and semi-healthy: a combination of protein, starch, and veggies with a side of fruit or dairy. Mix up the textures and flavors too; the worst brown-bag lunches, in my humble opinion, are those that offer no variety, and that's why people assume packing your lunch is dull and tasteless. You don't even have to cook if you'd rather not, but feel free to make something custom for lunch that feels special or that you know you'll like. I wouldn't go way out of your comfort zone here, either. Lunch is meant to be enjoyed, of course, but it's also just one meal of the day, and you don't need to overthink it.

BRING YOUR LUNCH EVERY DAY FOR A WEEK

For a solid week, see if you can avoid buying your lunch in favor of bringing it or eating at home. I can't promise all your meals will be very interesting—sorry, that's on you—but I can say that you'll most likely save money upward of at least $50, and you'll probably eat healthier too. It's just a week, so you can do this.

Along the way consider why you don't bring your lunch, or why you're so used to buying your lunch. Is it because of convenience or a crazy-busy schedule? Lack of knowledge or interest in preparing food or grocery shopping? Not sure what to make? Food from home seems cringeworthy in comparison to going out? You work hard, and picking up your lunch feels like a minor luxury since you can afford it anyway? There's no need to psychoanalyze your lunch habits, but it's worth thinking about your own motivations for bringing or buying lunch, and where you'd actually like to make a change. Maybe for you, going out for lunch on Fridays with your team is something you look forward to all week long. Or maybe you're never going to be the type of person who eats a sad desk lunch, and you need a change of scenery midday. You can use these reflections to figure out what combination of bringing and buying your lunch works best for you.

TRY THIS

This week experiment with four new ways you can bring your lunch to work. Try out a bento box for an adult-style Lunchable, eat outside instead of at your desk, make a custom burrito bowl rather than your standard salad, or repurpose leftovers so they don't go to waste. On Friday splurge and take yourself out to lunch as a reward.

USE THE 80/20 RULE FOR LUNCH

Although I enjoy bringing my lunch to work and eating at home most days, I also know that doing so every day gets old—and you gotta live a little. That's why on a monthly basis, I like the 80/20 rule: 80 percent of the time, I eat leftovers in my office, but the other 20 percent of the time, I give myself permission to buy a wrap from my favorite market down the street, head to the Whole Foods salad bar with a coworker, or grab a couple of tacos while out and about with my husband. This whole challenge isn't intended to prevent you from eating out or to make you feel bad about your decisions to do so. The goal is to adjust your mentality so that your norm doesn't equal takeout for every meal, and you can begin to explore cooking at home or prepping at least a couple of go-to meals on your own. Within the time frame of a month, you'll also begin to see how much eating out adds up financially, particularly if you take the extra step of adding up all those receipts. You might also notice a difference in how your clothes fit, in your energy levels depending on what you choose to eat for lunch (e.g., sodium-laden cheeseburger and fries versus a PB&J with carrot sticks on the side), and in how both impact what you eat for dinner and breakfast.

Know Your Health History

Whenever I go to the doctor and I'm asked about my family health history, my reply goes like this: "I think my mom's great-grandma had cancer...but I'm not sure what kind...and her grandfather had cancer, too, but he adopted her, so does that count? My dad has high blood pressure and is kinda depressed....I don't know if he takes medication, though?" (As if the doctor is going to confirm or deny these questions.) The point is that I'm never quite sure what to say, because health history isn't something I think about very often. I categorize it as stuff I can ask my parents when needed, but not information I actively need to know—and that's naive. When diseases and conditions like cancer, diabetes, Alzheimer's, and high blood pressure (among many others) exist in your family, that means your risk goes up, and you'll want to be mindful of any screenings, prevention tactics, or symptoms to watch for. Here's how to get the conversation going in terms of educating yourself on your own health history, figuring out where you may be at risk, and not taking your health for granted.

WRITE DOWN EVERYTHING YOU KNOW ABOUT YOUR HEALTH HISTORY

Start with the basics: what do you know about your immediate family members? That includes your parents, siblings, children, aunts and uncles, nieces and nephews, grandparents, and great-grandparents. Think of major medical issues, causes of death for those who have passed away, age upon diagnosis, any health risks related to your ethnicity, allergies, a history of birth defects or pregnancy loss, and so on. Then ask around to fill in the gaps, and if it feels weird to chat about health in this way, then remember you're trying to be proactive so you can look out for your own health and wellness.

Next figure out where you might be at risk. After a couple of conversations with my family, I quickly learned that depression, Alzheimer's, colon cancer, and high blood pressure all run in my family. That doesn't necessarily mean I'm going to experience each of those; it just means I need to be on the lookout for certain symptoms throughout my life as well as take steps to prevent or minimize my own risk. For example, I can make healthy choices now to minimize stress and anxiety. I can do crossword puzzles or other exercises to keep my memory strong. I can avoid smoking, drink alcohol in moderation, maintain a healthy weight, watch my salt intake, exercise, and eat a well-balanced diet. Will all of those actions ensure I will never suffer from any of the diseases that have affected my family members? No. But when you know better, you do better, and I'd rather do everything possible to protect my health than sit back and wait.

SPEND TIME WITH AN ELDERLY FRIEND OR FAMILY MEMBER

If you've mostly been healthy your whole life, then you might not think much about what happens when you get sick. But you will get sick, injured, or diagnosed with a condition—or if not you, someone you love. I don't say that to be depressing; I say that to emphasize the value of your own health. We humans spend an awful lot of time wishing our bodies and our lives were better in some way, but if you can breathe, and you can walk or run, and you can lift something heavy, and you can stretch your arms in the air, and you can wake up in the morning without taking a bunch of medication and go to sleep at night without pain—then you've got it good, my friend. And I think it's really important to practice gratitude for your mental and physical health on a daily, constant basis, because it's very easy to take it for granted.

The fastest way to practice this? Hang out with an elderly friend or family member. You'll pretty quickly learn that getting (and staying) in shape, watching what you eat to avoid conditions like high blood pressure or risk of diabetes, managing stress, and so on matter not simply for vanity's sake—but so you can live your best life for as many years as you're blessed to have. You're not invincible; nobody is. Spending time with those who carry a few more decades of knowledge and life experience under their belt is a good route to reminding yourself of this fact.

ACT ON YOUR HEALTH HISTORY

So you discover that your grandfather had colon cancer, your sister has breast cancer, and your mom has diabetes. What should you do with this knowledge? You should act on it. Talk to your doctor about your family history and then get yourself in line to do some early screenings for your specific risk factors. Having a family history of a disease automatically puts you in a place where you are more likely to get the same condition regardless of your current state of health. So act on it. If you have unhealthy habits like smoking, not exercising, or poor eating, then work to break or change them. Get regular screenings for the conditions your family history puts you at risk for, whether it be early mammograms, colonoscopies, bone screenings, genetic testing, or other medical preventative screenings. Do it even if you are apprehensive about the test. A few minutes of awkwardness is worth your life.

TRY THIS

Make four basic appointments to take care of yourself: visit a doctor, go to the dentist, and get your vision and hearing checked. Depending on your health history, educate yourself on any preventative measures you can currently explore at home or under the care of a medical professional—for example, if you've spent a lot of time in the sun and someone in your family had skin cancer, examine your body for any unusual moles or marks, and then find a local dermatologist. Be proactive about your health in the same way you'd take care of your home or vehicle: on an ongoing basis.

CHALLENGE #9:
Appreciate Your Body

The first time I thought about how much I weighed occurred in junior high. I liked a boy, and one of the mean girls in my class called me a string bean in front of him. Embarrassed, I bowed my head and immediately went home that day analyzing my body: my skinny arms, my long legs, my lack of boobs, my narrow nose. I wanted, more than anything, to be considered pretty—and right then, that meant having luscious curves and a full chest and being shorter than all the guys. In high school I recognized the benefits of a slender frame; I could be thrown into the air as a cheerleader, I fit into trendy size zero pants, and a high (i.e., teenage) metabolism allowed me to eat whatever I wanted with little impact to the scale. Once I arrived at college, things changed. I easily put on the freshman fifteen—twenty pounds, if we're being honest—and even though my weight technically still landed well within a normal range for my height, I felt uncomfortable taking up more space.

I spent the next decade unraveling those internalized expectations for how my body "should" look. While I still have days where a look in the mirror leads to a critical thought or two, I'm proud to finally feel like I've cultivated a true sense of body appreciation—and I'd love for you to be able to do the same. In this challenge you'll practice complimenting yourself, complimenting yourself around other people, and acknowledging what you like best about your body.

GIVE YOUR BODY ONE COMPLIMENT

Ever heard of "fat talk"? It's when you cycle through negative thoughts about your body and fall into a mental narrative sounding something like this: *My thighs are huge, I need to get rid of these jiggly bits, no wonder I can't get a date, I have frizzy hair, my life would be so much better if I just lost weight/had more muscles/fit into those jeans...* Delving into fat talk makes you feel terrible, even though you're doing it to yourself, and once you start, it's hard to stop.

If you're spiraling into fat talk, one of the best ways to hit the brakes is to give yourself a compliment. For example, tell yourself, "Wait, hold on. This isn't true. I actually like my thighs. They're strong and power-ful, and they help me run and walk and get to all the places I need to go." Here's the catch: whatever the compliment, it needs to be specific, and you have to genuinely mean it. None of this "Well, I guess I'm not ugly?" business. Really look at your physical self and question if what you're thinking, saying, and feeling is true—then find something to love about your body and say it out loud. If complimenting your body feels too challenging, you can even focus on something about yourself that's not physical at all, like your smarts or your kind heart or your work ethic or the fact that you're really good at making tacos. Just redirect your brain from something negative to something positive.

TELL SOMEONE ELSE ONE THING YOU LIKE ABOUT YOUR BODY

I used to believe that I wasn't strong. Not physically, anyway. Sure, I spent a decade as a ballet dancer and gymnast, but because I couldn't do a full push-up or run a mile under six minutes, I never viewed myself as a person with physical strength. It wasn't until I went through yoga teacher training that I realized how tightly I clung to this story line, and how strange it felt to let go.

We all internalize stories about our bodies, whether they're self-imposed, from society and culture at large, or old labels bestowed upon us by other people. Accepting your body is one thing. Openly acknowledging the gifts of your body to the outside world is a whole other ball game. Try this: take that compliment from the previous exercise, and see if you can share it with someone else. It's going to feel like you're bragging or breaking some sort of social rule that says we can't ever say anything nice about ourselves to other people, but you can do it. Be gracious and humble, but own what you love about your body—no excuses, no exceptions. What if you're like, "How do I ever work this into conversation?" You can open with "I'm working on accepting my body, and I want to try to say something nice about myself out loud in front of you. Can I try?"

EVERY DAY, ACKNOWLEDGE ONE THING YOU LIKE ABOUT YOUR BODY

When I'm feeling myself—eating right, working out consistently, fitting into favorite clothes—it's easier to appreciate my body. But when life gets in the way—living on chips and salsa, not moving from the couch, feeling soft in all the wrong places—I'm much more likely to talk shit about my body. This self-love stuff can be conditional, unfortunately, and it takes quite a bit of practice to remember to accept yourself and your body on a regular basis. It's also important to remember that your body is bound to change over the years; your size and shape may naturally fluctuate, and the goal of body positivity involves accepting yourself as you are. I've found that liking your body is actually less about the physical stuff (the number on the scale or what you look like in shorts) and much more about health and fitness (how fast you can run a mile, if you can recover from a bad cold). Redirect all the energy you used to spend on criticism to actually enjoying your life in a body that works. Then view your body as your friend, not your enemy, and treat it accordingly. If all else fails, think of the people you love: is it because of what they look like? Probably not. The same is true for you.

TRY THIS

For an entire month, find one thing to like about your body every day, and write it down on a sticky note for your bathroom mirror. This is probably the place where you check yourself out on a regular basis, so create a visual reminder of positive thoughts regarding your body. Remember, you're not examining yourself to locate things to "fix"; you're acknowledging what about your body you can respect and value right now. Let the sticky notes crowd your mirror, and at the end of the month, take a picture of the thirty or so compliments you've been able to give yourself. Save the photo, and look at this version of a mini gratitude journal whenever you're struggling with body appreciation.

Create Your Own Definition of Self-Care

What comes to mind when you think about self-care? Let me guess— some version of treat yo' self, including bubble baths and roses and glasses of wine and big bowls of ice cream and expensive massages. Maybe all of those things sound absolutely wonderful, and you can't wait. Or maybe you're more into the nap scene with a side of Cheetos and no emails to answer. Or maybe you like the concept of self-care, but you certainly don't have the funds or the time or the lifestyle or the energy to indulge like that.

I've been there. For something so seemingly straightforward, self-care can be sort of confusing, especially if you're always looking for a picture-perfect moment or feeling. Instead I think it's useful to determine your *own* definition of self-care so you can build out certain tactics and behaviors to use when you're needing a little love. We'll dive into how you can craft that definition as well as how you can schedule self-care into your ongoing routine.

FIGURE OUT WHAT SELF-CARE MEANS TO YOU

Self-care is a total buzzword these days. So set aside a little time to think about why self-care matters to *you* in the first place and what it might look like, in an ideal world, to support your needs. There's no right or perfect answer, and it might take you a while to come around to a few options. For me, self-care is all about giving myself an opportunity to pause and exist without the titles of mom, wife, sister, friend, employee, daughter, and so on. I frequently find myself on the hamster wheel of adult life, and then I look up all of a sudden, and I can't remember the last time I took a deep breath or stepped out of 24/7 reactive mode. I'm usually responding to the needs, questions, desires, and wants of others, and when I do something to take care of myself, it feels like a precious gift—and a reminder that I'm important too. Your definition may change over the course of a year, too, and that's okay, because it depends on what you need more or less of in a given period. For now, write it down in the form of an "I" statement: "I practice self-care by..." Then place that statement somewhere you can see it, like on the refrigerator or in your planner.

PICK ONE SELF-CARE ACTIVITY TO DO

Once I could identify my own definition of self-care, it became easier to notice the difference between weeks where I practiced it and weeks where I didn't. From there I could discern which types of activities fostered self-care moments, and which ones prevented me from being able to practice self-care at all. Let's take sleep. For me, getting enough sleep is a way to practice self-care. I'm a nicer person when I'm rested; when I don't get enough sleep, I'm not my best self. One of my self-care activities involves taking naps on the weekend with my son (#parentlife) and getting around seven hours of sleep per night during the week. But I also want to do other self-care things, too, like taking long, hot showers in the morning and eating a delicious dinner and going to yoga every day. The problem is I can't do it all, and if I try (even in the vein of self-care!), I turn into this perfection-striving wildebeest, which is no good for anyone, including myself.

So pick one thing to do this week, and don't fall into the trap of trying to do all the self-care things ever possible at your fingertips. Choose something that is accessible and makes you feel like a slightly better version of yourself.

TRY THIS

Making time for self-care isn't a luxury; it's a necessity. But it can be difficult to determine what you need in a given moment. To combat this, outline ten different ways you can practice self-care, and then identify why that activity matters to you and how it makes you feel when you do it. If "asking for help" is on your list, maybe that's because it allows you to feel "supported by your community" or "like you're not alone." "Cooking a healthy breakfast" might result in "feeling energized and healthy to start your day." Or "napping when the baby naps" is a way to "remember you don't have to be constantly productive." When you're teetering on the edge of making time for self-care, you can glance at your list and pick what you need most based on why that activity benefits you.

SCHEDULE SELF-CARE AS AN ESSENTIAL

One reason I think so many people struggle with self-care? They save it for special moments when they'll have more time or energy or money or...I don't know. It reminds me of the "side of the desk" phenomenon, when you push a project you're truly excited about off to the corner of your to-do list in favor of busywork, rather than making time and space for what lights you up inside. Like anything else, self-care isn't going to just magically happen; nobody is going to come to your house and hold your hand and say, "Now, honey, let's take care of ourselves, shall we?" (If that has indeed happened to you, I'm jealous of your life. Just saying.) You have to be the one to prioritize your own mental, physical, and emotional health, so start with one month and lay it all out there. Make it as normal as brushing your teeth.

I like to plan out a month of self-care based on my intentions, rather than worrying too much about what will or won't really happen. The framework is entirely up to you—you can simply own the mentality of "I need to do something for myself at least once a day" and play it by ear. You might prefer to pick three self-care things to do each week, whether they're the same or entirely different, and not necessarily assign each thing to a given day. Or maybe it's best for you to get down and dirty with the details, at least while you're getting started, by saying, "Monday: paint nails. Tuesday: go for a walk with the dog. Wednesday: eat a Popsicle. Thursday: watch pilot episode of new show. Friday: order pizza." But make yourself plan it out, or otherwise it likely won't happen. Be intentional, because you deserve to take care of yourself.

Part 3

Relationships

Therapist Esther Perel calls love an affirmation and a transcendence of who we are, an ideal that rests on two pillars: surrender and autonomy. In *Mating in Captivity*, she writes, "Today, we turn to one person to provide what an entire village once did: a sense of grounding, meaning, and continuity." Perel's work focuses on how committed, romantic love can be a place of great security and adventure—but at the same time, she acknowledges that our relationships with friends, kids, communities, parents, coworkers, and all kinds of other people in our lives are also valuable, meaningful, and complicated.

I'm no relationship expert, but I believe our connections to each other form the foundation of who we are, who we want to be, and who we become. My relationships, both past and current, serve as the source of my greatest joys and lowest lows. In this part we'll dive into some of the most impactful and useful lessons I've learned, as well as how you can begin to make tiny tweaks in some of your relationships to continue to grow as an individual. We'll talk about the importance of honesty, how to stop keeping score and be a better listener, why asking for (and accepting) help is so difficult, forgiveness and responsibility, and staying true to yourself.

CHALLENGE #1:
Tell the Truth

When I was a kid, my mom had one rule: be honest. I can still hear her saying, "If you tell me the truth, you might still get in trouble, but not as much as if you lie." After I naturally tested the limits of this particular family law—news flash, she wasn't kidding—it became an unspoken measuring stick regarding behavior and, even more so, how we communicated in our relationship as mother and daughter, parent and child. And in my mid-twenties, when I found myself chronically walking on the side of white lies and half-truths, her words were what led me back to the core of my own authenticity, my own straight and narrow.

Telling the truth matters; it's like water for the soul. So why do many of us resist or refrain from being fully honest in our relationships? We want true connection with others, so why do we stick to platitudes and small talk, or say we're fine when we're not, or withhold key pieces of information from our loved ones? I don't know. But in my experience, it's easy to veer away from truth-telling in our relationships for all kinds of silly and serious reasons, and I've made an ongoing effort to place honesty at the center. Here's what I've learned, and how you can use some of these same strategies to bring a bit more truth to your relationships as well.

RECOGNIZE THE FEELING OF WANTING TO FIB

For those of you who are like, "Lying is bad; don't do it!"—I get it. If telling the truth has always come easy to you, that's incredible—keep shining your light and setting a great example. However, I don't think it's that simple. Nobody *wants* to lie, not really, even if you know that honesty is the best policy. Lying feels shitty. But sometimes it also offers a temporary reprieve from a painful, difficult, or just slightly uncomfortable truth...and that's where many of us get tripped up. It can be as small as a white lie, like telling someone her hair looks great when it actually looks terrible, or saying you've read a popular book when you really haven't. It can be big, like lying to your spouse about where you were last night, or claiming to be over an argument while secretly holding a grudge. Lies can even be technically useful at times, especially to smooth over awkward moments or social situations. Still, I'd personally rather be knocked over by the truth than buoyed by a smooth lie.

It took me a long time, and a couple of years of therapy, to practice resisting that initial urge to slightly tweak the truth. Even now I'll run up against the desire to make a situation or myself look better than it really is. Then I'm reminded of how it feels to do so: like I'm hiding, like I'm disconnected from myself, like I'm looking over my shoulder, like I'm holding my own breath. And I don't want to feel that way, no matter how hard telling the truth might be.

Think about your own relationships. With whom do you feel the urge to tell a lie, big or small? What are the circumstances? Where does the impulse come from? How does it feel when you lie versus when you stick to the truth? Notice when you feel the urge to tell a lie, big or small. Try to take a moment to acknowledge the feeling, and then be as truthful as possible.

DITCH TOXIC FRIENDSHIPS

Hopefully you have a friendship in your life where you can be 100 percent yourself, no bullshit or facade. My friend Rachael is one of those people for me. We went to college together and then moved to Chicago, where we survived on hummus and crackers and cheap wine. We stood up in each other's weddings, and despite babies and cross-country moves and busy lives, we still manage to stay connected in a profound way. We have the type of friendship where you feel known and understood, where you can say what's on your mind without fear of judgment, where you trust the other person will always have your back but also won't hesitate to say things like "I think you're making a mistake" and "You really hurt my feelings" and "Why are you such a hot mess right now?" Even if we don't talk for a couple of weeks or months, when we do reconnect, there's a shared sense of vulnerability and honesty within our relationship. And that's what enables us to continue to grow as individuals, and as good friends, as the years go by.

Without honesty, relationships become toxic. That label might seem reserved for fake friends or bullies, but any friendship where dishonesty, drama, gossip, or meanness reigns supreme isn't one built on emotional honesty. Take a good look at your friendships, and identify which ones lift you up and which ones bring you down. For the latter, do your best to distance or remove yourself from any person with whom honesty is a missing piece of the puzzle. Another option? If you really don't want to lose the relationship in question, try to talk to that individual about why you need more truth-telling within the context of your connection, and how you both can contribute to making that happen.

TELL THE TRUTH, EVEN IF IT'S HARD TRUTH

Raise your hand if you know someone who starts most sentences with "If I'm being honest..." or "I don't wanna be rude, but..." only to proceed to say something honest but harsh, and most *definitely* rude. Heck, maybe you've been that person before. In my opinion this is where relationships fail, because they aren't a safe space for truth-telling. Honesty requires openness absolutely but also an ability to hold space for another person with a spark of courage and a hefty dose of compassion, rather than criticism rooted in assumptions or expectations. It's not about being right, and not about feeling as though you "know better" (even if you do!).

It's about speaking truth in a way that matters so your relationship can grow. This requires a great deal of trial and error, and can be emotionally demanding too. When I think back on some of the most powerful conversations I've had in a relationship with someone I cared about, many of them involved discussing a truth that hurt. Being honest means you're willing to both say hard things and hear hard things, and sometimes it involves the demise or destruction of the relationship at stake. Here's the alternative, though—if you don't tell the truth, especially with the people you love, you can never experience the type of relationship you're probably looking for in the first place: one built on mutual trust, communication, and respect.

TRY THIS

For the next week, in all your interactions, do a gut check before opening your mouth. Ask yourself, "Am I telling the truth? And if not, why?" Another useful phrase is this: "Does this make me look good or feel good right now?" Dishonesty tends to root itself in controlling what other people think of us, and attempting to warp reality to fit the mode of who or what we "should" be. You'll know, deep down, when you're twisting the truth to look good. And even if the truth at hand is complicated or painful, which sucks, it always feels better in the long run to err on the side of honesty.

CHALLENGE #2:
Stop Keeping Score

Before my husband and I had our first child, an older relative gave us a piece of advice: "Be on the same team." We sort of chuckled at the time—I mean, obviously we were on the same team; we're married and about to welcome a kid into our lives. A season later, as we bickered about who was more tired after being up with the baby and whose turn it was to do the dishes, I realized what our relative meant. Being on the same team? Harder than I thought. We were cultivating an attitude of getting versus giving, which didn't lead anywhere healthy; instead it created friction in our marriage because we each constantly felt like we were contributing more than the other person. Things weren't "fair," and that felt frustrating.

Actively choosing to be on the same team as your partner is actually... much harder than it seems. And sliding into the territory of tallying who does what and how often against an imaginary scoreboard is probably the fastest journey to relationship resentment possible. Here's how to shift that toxic mind-set for good, clear lingering scorecards, and maintain a "nobody wins" mind-set that'll keep you in check.

CLEAR THE SCORECARD

On my Cleaning the Bathroom Toilet scorecard, I've got about a hundred marks and my husband has, I don't know, maybe one? At least that's how it feels. And every time I notice the toilet needs to be cleaned, I think about how I'm typically the one who cleans it. Sometimes I'll make little funny-but-not-really comments to him, like "Wow, this bathroom is so filthy; how can you be in here without noticing?" Just to see if he'll magically offer, in that exact moment, to grab the bleach wipes and go to town. (Update: hasn't happened yet.) Sometimes I'll avoid cleaning for as long as possible, in a silent battle of will-he-or-won't-he. (Update: he won't, and I'm the only one who cares.) Eventually I get to a point where I clean the freaking bathroom because...whatever. He does plenty of stuff around the house that I don't do and don't care about, like taking the trash out and fixing our Internet every time it breaks.

You can keep score for as long as you like, but at some point you'll be sick of it, or at least sick of _thinking_ about it. No matter who the relationship is with, sooner or later you arrive at a crossroads of "Do I care about this anymore?" If yes, keep fighting that battle. But my advice, generally speaking, is to wipe the slate clean regarding minor issues. For a day, just let go of the little things that you keep tallying as evidence of who does more. Stop keeping score in your own head, and imagine that you're starting over with grace and goodwill.

TRACK EACH INSTANCE OF "NEVER" AND "ALWAYS"

Actual conversation I had with my husband:

"I just feel like I'm always in charge of dinner, and you never help out..."

"You never asked me to help!"

"Why do I have to ask? Can't you just do it?"

Trade out dinner for daycare pickup, sex, paying bills, cleaning, literally *anything*, and you've got a conversation that probably sounds pretty familiar to most couples. Words like "never" and "always" tend to creep into relationship conflicts like splinters. When those words pop up, everyone's first line of defense is attack mode. It is also rare to find a "never" or "always" conversation that rings completely true. My claim that I always make dinner and my husband never helps? Not true. However, it's easy for me to forget in the heat of the moment when I'm overwhelmed.

This week, rather than tracking points regarding who does what in a relationship, pay attention to how often you say "never" and "always." When you catch yourself using those words, pause and reframe your language in a way that's less absolute. For example, "You never do the dishes" could be rephrased as "From my lens, I usually do the dishes, and I'd really appreciate it if you tackled them a few more nights a week." This approach is more solution-oriented versus just blaming the other person, which promotes healthy communication and better manages expectations all around.

TRY THIS

You've probably heard of a "swear jar," where you put money in a container every time you let a curse word slip. Do the same thing for "never" and "always." Get two jars, label them accordingly, and put them in a visible location at home. Every time you or your partner says "never" or "always," put a dollar in the jar—and then rephrase what you're trying to say. After the jar fills up (or a predetermined period of time, like a week or a month), go on a date using the money.

STOP TRYING TO "WIN"

Keeping score either makes me feel super righteous regarding what the other person "should" be doing or indignantly awaiting my gold stars for what I'm doing "right," until I remember that there are no winners in this game. Case in point: our newborn son didn't care one bit that one parent got more sleep than the other, and that the dishes sat in the sink until somebody ultimately put them in the dishwasher. Our arguing over both topics led to no winners, just two tired parents trying to survive a baby and a messy home. The only thing that matters, then, is *being on the same team*. When you're on the same team, you assume that everybody else is pulling their weight, and you know each player brings different strengths and skill sets to the field. You trust each other, and you give each other the benefit of the doubt. There's no "I" in "we," and you don't win any trophies by trying to do it all by yourself. You don't make your teammates feel like they're not good enough, and you don't act like you're the best.

This month, instead of keeping score for all the ways in which someone lets you down or doesn't meet your expectations, stop trying to win. Own up to any shortcomings you might have, and try to view giving as a gift you're able to offer another person.

CHALLENGE #3:
Be a Better Listener

Over the years in my career, I noticed something about the leaders and bosses I admired. No matter how busy they were, if I stopped by for a meeting or to ask a question, they stopped and listened. They didn't multitask while saying "Uh huh, go on," or glance at their watches or phones, or act impatient. They didn't look over my shoulder to see if there was someone better or more essential to talk to down the hall. They acted like they had all the time in the world to hear what I had to say, like it was important to them. I also worked with people who behaved oppositely, which unsurprisingly made me feel insignificant, hesitant, and disrespected.

The average human supposedly has an eight-second attention span. Combine that with the reality of endless opportunities for distraction, and our ability to be present and stay focused on one thing at a time is drastically affected. It requires discipline to counteract this shiny object syndrome, and one way to practice involves honing your ability to listen.

STOP THINKING ABOUT WHAT YOU'RE GOING TO SAY NEXT

My dad is famous for asking someone a question, then about midway through the answer, changing the subject to another topic. It's not that he's trying to be rude; he's just not the best listener and his mind runs a million miles a minute, which has become a running joke in our family. I've learned to laugh about it and gently call him out, but in general I'm aware that when you're the person on the receiving end of that kind of behavior, it doesn't feel good.

When you spend the majority of your verbal interactions with other people planning what you'll say and do next, you're being self-centered, even if that's not your intent. You're effectively telling yourself, and the person involved, that your thoughts and words and perspective matter most and, as a result, should receive the most airtime. And by doing this, you're not only unable to hear what the other person has to say, but there's also no space for useful information sharing, growth, or connection in terms of the relationship being built.

Today, in every conversation, instead of thinking about what you're going to say next, focus on listening to the other person. Don't rehearse what you'll say in advance, tune out, interrupt, or even anticipate what you think the other person is going to say. Listen fully, like an engaged participant in a two-way exchange—you know, the way it's supposed to be when you're communicating with someone.

SINGLE-TASK INSTEAD OF MULTITASK

Picture this: you're on the phone with someone or in a group meeting and simultaneously jotting down notes, checking your email, and thinking about what's for dinner. Seems fine, right? If someone were to call you out in that situation for multitasking, you'd probably react defensively: "I'm listening, I swear! I'm really good at doing two things at once. I'm making the best use of my time—besides, I'm just sitting here anyway." And you'd be wrong.

Nobody is "good" at multitasking. While multitasking is a necessary skill, at times, for managing tasks and responsibilities in your professional and personal life, it shouldn't be your default approach to every situation because it forces your brain to do several things at once. Even though you think you're performing at high capacity in this way, it's more likely you're half-assing each thing you're trying to do, which takes more time and energy in the long run. On average, says University of California distraction expert Gloria Mark, it takes about twenty-five minutes to return to your original task after an interruption—and when you're multitasking, you're basically interrupting *yourself* over and over. It's also ridiculously apparent when someone is multitasking right in front of you, whether he's typing away on a laptop while nodding emphatically or listening to you with a dead-eyed expression.

Try to single-task in an effort to be fully present, bringing your best energy to a situation or a person. Show up in conversations, and notice when others don't—and how it makes you feel as a result.

TRY THIS

This week practice single-tasking in every interaction, meeting, or conversation. If you're on the phone, keep your mind focused on that; if you're making dinner, stop simultaneously cleaning the kitchen and reading your email. Come up with a phrase to keep you on track, such as "one thing at a time," "slow down," "pay attention," or my personal favorite, "eye contact."

USE THE 2:1 RATIO

Have you ever been in a conversation where it's hard to get a word in edgewise? It's fine once in a while, particularly if the other person clearly needs to vent or tell a long story, but in most conversations it's nice to have a bit of back-and-forth. From a listening perspective, that's where this rule can be helpful: listen twice as much as you talk. Scott Eblin, the author of *Overworked and Overwhelmed: The Mindfulness Alternative*, calls this the 2:1 ratio. You can also practice holding a "thinking" mind-set versus a "doing" mind-set—in other words, your conversation isn't necessarily an item to check off your to-do list, but an opportunity to actively learn or connect.

This month practice the 2:1 ratio in as many conversations as possible. Observe where you're anxious to pipe up, and try to listen in that moment instead. Ask thoughtful questions to show you're listening and open to receiving the information being shared. Be genuinely interested in what the other person is saying, and allow yourself to feel surprised by what comes up—maybe it's different than what you expected.

Ask for (and Accept) Help

For the longest time, admitting I needed help—and accepting help from other people, whether acquaintances, coworkers, close friends, or loved ones—left me fraught with emotions. I didn't want to look weak or silly, or impose on someone and seem too needy; I wanted to appear like I had it all together, like I didn't need anything from anyone, because that's what I thought strong people did. Even if I was struggling, I kept trying to prove to myself that I could handle "it," whatever "it" happened to be: a bad day, childcare, work projects, moving furniture. And when a person happened to break through my wall of "Everything is fine! I'm fine!" I would quickly backtrack to a place of savage independence: "No, no, it's okay, I've got it." Which honestly made my life even harder, and probably annoyed the heck out of the people who were trying so hard to support me.

What's up with our collective discomfort around asking for and accepting help? We're human, and we're built to rely on each other. Here's how to incorporate more of the yin and yang of giving and receiving into your life.

ASK FOR HELP WITH ONE THING

Under pressure I'm apt to claim I can handle anything and everything. It's taken me a long time to realize just because I *can* doesn't mean that I *should* or that I *have* to. For example, if we need a babysitter for our son, my sister is one of the first people to volunteer. She and I have an amazingly close relationship, which I'm so thankful for, and she also happens to live five minutes away. And my kiddo adores her. Yet somehow I still feel this uneasy stress: "Am I inconveniencing her? Does she *really* want to watch him? I'm sure she's busy, I mean, I can probably just make it work..." And this is after she's already said yes! It's like I'm bombarded with this lingering sense that I "should" be able to do everything on my own without needing help, which is silly.

One thing you can do every day to make your life a little bit better? Ask for help, even if it's something you could technically tackle if necessary. At the office ask your coworker to take the assignment, support you on a project, or offer a potential solution to a problem you've been mulling over. At home ask your partner or parent to do the dishes or handle bedtime, a friend or sibling to mow your lawn or pick up your prescription. Enlist your kids to pick up their toys, your neighbors to bring in your mail, and that stranger at the store to hold the door for you. It might feel a little weird, admitting that a single act can lift you up, but that's what community—and being in relationships with other people—means.

ACCEPT AN OFFER OF HELP

My friend Haverlee and I were out for drinks one time, and this topic of asking for and accepting help came up. She said something like, "It's nice to be on the receiving end of help, but I wish more people realized how good it feels to be able to help. It's like a gift you can give, and saying no to someone's offer to help prevents them from feeling that joy." Her comments stuck with me—I had forgotten how lovely it feels to support someone, even in a small way.

The next time you encounter a version of "Can I help you with any-thing?" say yes. Say yes to the store clerk who wants to know if you've found everything you're looking for; sure, you could locate the chips on your own, but why not let her lead the way? Say yes to the person in your life who volunteers to bring over wine or pick up dinner after you've had a long day. Say yes to the friend who asks if you need to talk, because you know what? You kinda do. Let people care for you in major and minor actions without feeling like you owe them or you "should" be able to do whatever it is. Needing help doesn't make you a needy person, nor is it a sign of weakness. You'll always have the opportunity to go it alone; don't preemptively walk the road of life by yourself. Give other people the opportunity to feel good by helping *you*.

TRY THIS

This week accept help whenever it is offered without feeling embarrassed or guilty. The grocery store clerk says he'll carry your bags out to your car, if you want? Say yes. Your friend asks if she can help clean up after a dinner party at your house? Take her up on it. Your coworker proposes working together on a stressful project with a tight deadline? Accept the support. These little moments of receiving help grant you the chance to connect with others in a powerful way.

MAKE A LIST OF THE THINGS YOU NEED HELP WITH AND ASSIGN THE TASKS TO OTHERS

My husband isn't the type to preemptively say, "Hey, what do you need help with this week?" It's just not in his DNA. However, if I say, "I really need help with..." he's more than willing to lend a hand and step up, no questions asked. This dynamic used to drive me nuts—I wanted him to read my mind, notice when I clearly had taken on too much, and pipe up. Then I realized this mentality wasn't exactly fair (or realistic) and, more importantly, didn't require any effort on my end other than stewing in resentment, waiting for him to identify the exact moments when I needed support. It turns out, for me, the very act of asking him for help *before* he offers is the real challenge. Because I don't like to ask. I want to be Superwoman, and asking for help feels like I'm really saying, "It's too much, I can't do this without you, I need you." To be incredibly honest, it makes me feel exceptionally vulnerable, but it's also a stitch that draws us together. I think of all the times he's asked me for help or support, and how honored I felt to be there for him. So why do I resist waving a white flag, especially with someone who is clearly in my corner?

Here's a thing about other people: they're not mind readers. If you're going through a tough time or even just having a bad day, and someone offers to help you, say yes! When people say, "Let me know how I can help," they're usually sincere in their offer—but the offer (and the help) can fade away because they are not sure exactly what you need or want. And do you know why they aren't sure? Because you never told them! If someone offers you help, assign that person a task to help with. Not only will it be one thing off your plate, but your friend also will feel like she is genuinely helping you, which is all she wants to do.

This month make a list of everything you need help with. Then try proactively asking for help with those items, and make sure you accept the help when someone offers!

CHALLENGE #5:
Forgive Someone

I once fell in love with someone, and our on-again, off-again relationship seemed equal parts struggle and passion. When we weren't trying to be together, we dated other people—sometimes seriously, sometimes not—which led to a whole host of complicated emotions. After a particularly fraught decision to take a break (his choice, not mine), I remember seeing him walk down the street with a woman we both worked with who he swore up and down was "just a friend." You can imagine where this is going: long story short, all that time they weren't "just friends," and I didn't learn the truth until many years later.

This man and I hurt each other in so many ways. But that very specific detail, that image of the two of them walking closely, stuck with me for an exceptionally long time as something I couldn't forgive, couldn't get over—even as our story eventually ended, and after we both moved on to happier and healthier relationships. And holding onto that righteous resentment did me exactly zero favors.

That's why forgiveness matters. Without it, you're floundering under the thumb of pain and bitterness, and nobody stays hurt except you. I certainly can't speak for everyone, but in my opinion, the act of forgiving ranks as one of the most challenging decisions a person can make; it requires an acceptance of the past, a realization of what you can't change or control, and a dedication to moving forward, even if you never forget the thing that happened to you. But when you practice forgiveness, with yourself or another person, you also find freedom.

FORGIVE SOMEONE WHO HURT YOU

When it was time to walk down the aisle at my wedding, my grandparents were nowhere to be found, until a friend hustled them to my side. During the reception I could barely find my grandma, as she mostly flitted around complaining to family members about the heat of the September evening. My grandpa said one thing to me—that I should "cover up a little" based on the V-neck cut of my gown.

It's not like I had a historically negative relationship with my grandparents, either—we typically got along well. But for whatever reason that year, they dropped the ball and didn't show up for me in the way I expected. I loved them with all my heart, and they not only pissed me off but also completely disappointed me. I remember how mad and hurt I felt at their behavior, and those emotions sunk their claws into my heart and directly impacted our relationship. Then one day it mattered a little less. And a little less. And a little less. And I finally chose to forgive them—not because I didn't care about the way they acted, but because it didn't feel worth holding onto anymore.

Think about someone who hurt you, and consider what it would be like to forgive that person. Tell him in person or in an email, a phone call, or a text. Or merely practice forgiving the person over and over again, until you start to let it go. I know forgiveness is not easy. But ultimately I've learned you can't control other people; you can only control how you react to them.

TRY THIS

Actively think of one person you need to forgive; this may be someone in your present or from your past, a stranger or a loved one. Write down the person's name on a piece of paper, along with what she did to harm you. Say out loud, "I forgive you," and take a deep breath. Do this a couple of times, and then burn, tear up, or throw away the paper as an act of letting go.

RELEASE A GRUDGE (MAJOR OR MINOR)

One thing I find really laughable about human behavior is our insistence on telling people we are *over* a certain situation when we're so clearly *not*. Why do we do this? Maybe it's because we're trying to fake it till we make it. Or maybe we like the feeling of secret anger as we wait for it to be acknowledged or resolved by the other person. Or maybe we know our little grudge is silly, and we're annoyed with ourselves for hanging onto it. Or we can't pinpoint exactly why we're upset in the first place. I'm not sure. I do know that when you're holding a grudge, you're also gripping an expectation around being "owed" something or a desire to "get even." Obviously this mind-set rarely works out well for anyone.

Holding a grudge has been shown to take a negative physical toll, not only on your mental health but on your body as well. People joke about problems or issues being a "weight" on their mind, because long-standing grudges can increase stress and negative emotions like anger and resentment. It can also lead to increased risks for ulcers, heart disease, and high blood pressure. So let it go—either speak up and tell the person you're holding a grudge against exactly how he has injured you, or decide to release the hurt on your own and move on. Neither option is easy, and both can be fraught with potential pitfalls. However, if you continue to hold onto the grudge, you're only hurting yourself.

FORGIVE YOURSELF FOR A TIME YOU MESSED UP

That man I mentioned at the beginning of this challenge who broke my heart? Well, I broke his too. There were moments in that relationship when I acted like my worst self; I lied, I manipulated, and I played dirty. But when someone hurts you, it's easy to play the victim and focus on what they did *to* you versus any potential role you may have had. Even if you manage to forgive that person for their words or actions, it's even harder to forgive yourself. I'm not perfect, and I've done and said things I fully regret, things that make me want to cover my face with my hands and hide. Things that make me feel like I'm not worthy of love, or compassion, or even grace. I'm willing to bet there's something in your life that might make you feel the same way, and I'm here to tell you it's okay to go ahead and forgive yourself.

Next time that negative voice in your head or heart starts chirping about how you're a failure, you messed up, you're not good enough, you missed the boat...say to yourself, "I forgive you." Pretend like you're a toddler trying to learn how to walk; you'll get it eventually, but you're going to trip and scrape your knee—and scream at the people who love you—along the way. Offer yourself a big handful of mercy with a dose of kindness.

CHALLENGE #6:
Take Responsibility

When I was growing up, if my mom happened to be in a bad mood about something, my dad often shrugged his shoulders like, "Oh well." And vice versa—if my dad was in a bad mood, then my mom basically said, "Your mood, your problem; don't take it out on the rest of us." I viewed this dynamic as a little strange. Weren't you *supposed* to be concerned with the feelings of the person you loved? Then I got married, and I realized I had it all wrong. As much as I genuinely wanted to bring warmth and joy and positivity to my husband's life, I also knew it wasn't my job to make him happy. I promised to love and cherish him, for better or worse, and I would do everything in my power to lift him up and support his needs, but at the end of the day, I can control only my words, my actions, my attitude. And he's in charge of his.

Relationships often seem like a thing that happens *to* us, and love is usually depicted as an item we receive. No wonder many of us spend our waking hours looking at our spouses and friends and siblings, thinking some version of *So what are you going to do for me today?* Meaning: what am I getting (or not getting) out of this exchange? But healthy, strong relationships don't necessarily function that way. They're not transactional in terms of receiving and reacting and controlling; they're living, growing entities that require care and attention. This challenge is all about relational responsibilities: how much you should expect to give, why you need to keep your side of the street clean, and ways to be responsible for the energy you bring to the room.

GIVE 100 PERCENT TO
GET 100 PERCENT

For a long time, I approached romantic relationships with an "if, then" mind-set: if I gave 50 percent, then I expected the other person to give 50 percent as well, and from there I assumed we'd find some sort of love balance or power equilibrium. Unsurprisingly this attitude didn't get me very far, mostly because I operated out of a desire to protect myself from pain and prepare for the worst. I didn't want to get hurt or be disappointed, and so I kept one foot out the door as a way to avoid being 100 percent invested— even though I desperately wanted to love and be loved. I thought I was practicing "give-and-take" in my relationships, but I actually had it backward.

According to couples who have been married for decades, lasting, happy partnerships require a ratio of 100/100, not 50/50. When both people give 100 percent every single day, in terms of attitude and communication and effort, relationships are more likely to be physically, emotionally, and mentally fulfilling. It's kind of similar to how babies and toddlers need a lot of sleep in order to sleep well at night; the more love you receive in a relationship, the higher your potential to be able to give love back to the other person. Dr. Phil McGraw of the famed *Dr. Phil* show seconds this concept; he believes we are each responsible for what we bring to a relationship, how we feel, and what we maintain or allow from our partners. In other words, you need a mind-set of abundance rather than scarcity: give 100 percent with the expectation that your partner will do the same, and ideally that's how both of you get your needs met.

TRY THIS

Think of one small action you can do today that would either show love to a person you care about or make the person's life a smidgen easier. Maybe it's a quick note of appreciation, taking out the trash without being asked, or bringing coffee in bed. If you're not sure, ask! The person might be pleasantly surprised and hopefully return the favor in the future.

KEEP YOUR SIDE OF THE STREET CLEAN

Alcoholics Anonymous has a tenet about keeping your side of the street clean, and while it is intended to help those struggling with addiction stay focused on their own recovery, there are some parallels to taking responsibility for your own actions first and foremost. Imagine you live in a house, and one day you look out the window and see a bunch of junk on your lawn. You go outside and clean it up. The next day you look out the window, and this time there's junk on your lawn *and* your neighbor's lawn. You clean up your lawn and wait for your neighbors to do the same. Except they don't. You can wonder why it's taking so long, push them to get started, and feel uber annoyed by the entire thing, but ultimately your job is to *keep your* side of the street clean.

When you take responsibility in your relationships, it means making choices with integrity, but it also means you're in charge of how much time or energy you devote to each interaction or situation. You can't control the way other people behave, not in the long run, but you can control the way you behave: practicing honest communication, skipping the blame game, finding solutions, making choices with integrity, rooting yourself in love. Keeping your side of the street clean relieves stress, because it ultimately allows you to stay in alignment with who you are and who you want to be.

BE RESPONSIBLE FOR THE ENERGY YOU BRING INTO A ROOM

Brain scientist Dr. Jill Bolte Taylor suffered a massive stroke at age thirty-seven, and in her book *My Stroke of Insight*, she writes about being in the hospital afterward, completely aware of the energy each nurse brought into the room—even though she couldn't talk or see. Some moved in and out, touching her hastily to check vitals then moving on to the next patient, and others made the effort to speak gently and pat her foot or shoulder. After she recovered and began to share her story years later, Dr. Taylor emphasized that each person who cared for her brought a certain energy into the space, and those who brought positivity and warmth and healing helped her much more than those who were negative or distracted or stressed out.

I once interviewed a doctor about leadership habits who said the same thing. As a leader he knew that every time he stepped into a room with his team members, he brought the energy either up or down. If he had a bad day, was running late, felt frustrated by an unrelated situation, or gave a distant hello while swiping on his phone—that set the tone with his team. And if he chose to put all of that aside in favor of a welcoming greeting, enthusiasm about the work ahead, eye contact, and promptness—that also set the tone. He told me that you get to decide, every day, which road you want to take. It's your responsibility to set the tone, and that has a trickle-down effect in terms of impacting other people.

Think about what energy you bring to a room or a relationship. Take responsibility for the way you want to show up.

Learn How to Apologize

When a child does something that requires apologizing, like throwing his toys or shoving a little friend at daycare, we make him say, "I'm sorry." It's the so-called right thing to do as a parent, but as any parent knows, a forced apology means zilch. Over time he'll learn that certain actions result in needing to say those words, so he'll likely throw out the phrase, almost automatically, to resolve an issue, make a problem go away, or heal a relationship. I know this because the same is true for adults too.

It's really easy to put forth an insincere apology and much harder to train yourself to apologize properly, but the latter can absolutely be done. I'm not talking about trivial apologies either, like knocking a cup of milk over or accidentally locking the garage door; we're focusing on the hard stuff here. Apologizing is a trait everyone can benefit from honing—so even if you think you're "good" at apologizing, try the three exercises outlined in this challenge to sharpen your skills.

RECOGNIZE THE DIFFERENCE BETWEEN A GOOD APOLOGY AND A BAD ONE

DIFFICULTY LEVEL: EASY

Think about a previous experience where you received an apology that either felt really powerful and meaningful, or didn't resolve an issue in the least. It's very clear when someone *sounds* like he's apologizing, but he also happens to be justifying, blaming, making excuses, or minimizing.

- "I'm sorry, but you were..."
- "Well, I'm sorry you feel that way..."
- "I'm sorry, I had a headache and..."
- "I was just kidding, geez, sorry..."

Add that it was probably accompanied by a huffy tone, crossed arms, or an eye roll, and you guessed it: nothing was resolved and nobody felt better.

In contrast, JoEllen Poon, former teacher and author of the *Cuppacocoa* parenting blog, says good apologies need to be specific, understanding, action-oriented, and reconciliation-oriented. She offers this framework, which is meant to be used in this order: *I'm sorry for... This is wrong because... In the future, I will... Will you forgive me?*

Now a good apology doesn't need to use those exact sentence prompts, but it does need to include the same sentiments: acknowledging what you did wrong, why it was wrong, what you'll do differently going forward, and a request for forgiveness.

PRACTICE SAYING "I'M SORRY" WITH THE BODY LANGUAGE TO MATCH

Apologies make people nervous or awkward, hence the rambling explanations and excuses. You may not even realize you're doing it. Unlike the easy challenge, where you're working to be mindful rather than defensive, sometimes we talk "around" an apology with the best intentions. But a true apology requires you to say the words "I'm sorry," full stop, out loud. For example, my sisters and I once teased our mom so much that she started crying. We immediately felt terrible because our intent was all in good fun, and we certainly didn't mean to actually hurt her feelings. I remember feeling surprised that she got so upset and consequently asked a bunch of questions about why, all while staring out the window and giving my sisters raised eyebrows—but I really just needed to look her in the eye and say "I'm sorry," regardless of the "why." Once we finally did that, my mom felt better and forgave us, and we all moved on and had a nice day together.

Practice giving an authentic apology with someone you trust, like a friend, coworker, or family member. Watch your body language: maintain eye contact, keep a neutral face (no grimacing or smiling!), and relax your arms and hands at your side. Ask the person you're practicing with to give you feedback on your words and actions. The goal isn't to avoid ever having to deliver an apology—that's not realistic, because everyone makes mistakes—but to be prepared so you can say "I'm sorry" and mean it.

APOLOGIZE THE RIGHT WAY AND ASK THE SAME OF OTHERS

DIFFICULTY LEVEL:

HARD

The other week I snapped at my husband for being on his phone while playing with our son. "Can you just put your phone down, please?" I asked in a huff. "I was just looking at the Cardinals score!" he retorted. "Okay," I said, as I shut the pantry door with a bang. "I just would prefer if you paid attention to our kid when he's trying to hang out with you and you haven't seen him all day."

Yikes. Them's fighting words, and I knew it right away. I knew I needed to apologize—my observation wasn't wrong necessarily, but I could've brought it up in a much more respectful way.

"Hey, I'm sorry for what I said about being on your phone," I ventured. "It's okay," he replied. Knowing my husband, that's when I could've easily left it alone, but I forced myself to continue with a real apology. I explained that I saw him on his phone and jumped to conclusions about what he was doing. I also was feeling a little guilty about being on my computer earlier, and I took that out on him based on an unfair expectation that we as parents needed to be 100 percent present 100 percent of the time. He agreed, and we hugged and moved on.

Effective apologies force you to admit fault and swallow your ego, which can be uncomfortable even with those who know you best, but without them relationships can't heal from major and minor rifts. So start apologizing the right way whenever possible. Say "I'm sorry" without going through the motions to get it over with, without sliding into one million reasons for your behavior, without obsessing over how the other person may respond. Focus on the fact that you made a mistake and caused pain to someone you care about.

TRY THIS

Think about an apology you'd like to "redo." Ask the person in question if you can revisit the past issue at stake, even if it's completely resolved, and explain that you would appreciate the chance to apologize properly. Then use JoEllen Poon's four-part apology structure to give that relationship a fresh start.

CHALLENGE #8:

Stay Curious, Not Furious

I once heard Adam Carroll, a transformational speaker and financial expert, speak at a work retreat about fixed and growth mind-sets, a concept dissected by all sorts of teachers and doctors and professional coaches. But he mentioned a phrase that stuck with me: stay curious, not furious. In all of our relationships, he continued, some modicum of conflict or discomfort is healthy and expected; however, when you're at odds with someone or run into negativity in your own state of mind, it's best to foster a reaction of curiosity. Because that's how you learn and grow, even if growing in that particular moment (or in that particular way) doesn't look exactly how you planned.

CHECK YOUR ASSUMPTIONS

A friend and I were going through a period where we didn't talk much. Our lives were on two different paths—her media career required long hours, and as a working mom, time on my end felt scarce. I was upset with the state of our friendship. I assumed that she didn't care as much, and our friendship would suffer as a result.

Then I happened to be heading to her town for a family event, so I texted her and said, "Are you around early Saturday morning? I can bring over coffee." I showed up and we sat on her couch and talked for two hours. I thought it might be a little weird, considering we hadn't really connected in six months, but it wasn't. Instead I learned all sorts of updates about her life, things that were too complex to put in a text or an email or a phone call. I watched her facial expressions dance as she told me different stories, and she listened carefully when I shared my own. When I left that day, I felt more reconnected to her than I had in a year, something I didn't expect that day—however, none of that would've happened if I hadn't reached out and let go of my assumptions.

In the book *The Four Agreements*, Don Miguel Ruiz says it's human nature to equate our assumptions with the truth, take other people's words and actions personally, and create a bunch of drama for no reason. Why? Because we think everybody else sees the world the same way we do. We think that other people know exactly what we mean, and that we know what they mean. But this is often where miscommunication thrives, which prevents us from connecting with others.

TRY THIS

The next time you make an assumption, use one of the following frameworks to ask a question instead: "What did you mean when you said...?" or "Why do you feel that way?" Seek to gather some evidence so you can actually test your assumption at hand. Maybe you're right, but maybe not. You may find that you learn much more this way too!

OBSERVE YOUR REACTIONS

In our neighborhood we're surrounded by several couples who have lived on the same block for years and years. They know each other well, and they're quite a bit older than us. When we moved into our house, they welcomed us with open arms, and we soon learned that they love to socialize: games, dinner outings, holiday celebrations, and most regularly, Friday porch nights, where someone puts up a flag and everybody comes over for a beer, snacks, and some end-of-week chitchat. The first couple of times we went, it was nice. And then I started to resent going every Friday. *Fridays are my time!* I whined to myself. *I've worked hard all week, I'm tired, I just want to chill at home with my family, I don't feel like social-izing with a bunch of people who aren't in my inner circle,* etc. Every week when I saw the flag, the exasperation bubbled about going over there, even though nobody was forcing me to.

During one particular episode, I managed to hit the brakes on my thoughts for a second. *Why am I so worked up over this?* I thought, gen-uinely curious. *Who cares if they want to hang out every Friday? If I want to go, I'll go, and if not, no big deal. Why is this making me so mad?* Why indeed. Upon a little more introspection, I realized it had nothing to do with them (shocker). My irritation belied guilt: I felt bad when I didn't go over there, as though it made me look like a "bad" neighbor, and I felt conflicted between wanting to seem like a "good" neighbor and also really valuing my chill time at home on Friday nights. After observing my reactions for weeks on end, I finally figured out why I got all out of shape about something so small, and it helped me shift out of a completely unnecessary funk.

The next time you find yourself overanxious, overly frustrated, or overly emotional about a person or a situation, observe your reactions and invite some curiosity around whatever emotions come up.

PRACTICE CURIOSITY IN A CONFLICT

My colleague and I were working on a new project that required a shared calendar tool, and after months of research, we finally had it nailed down to the perfect option for our team. Then we ran into a tiny glitch and reached out to our IT department, who told us we needed to use a different platform—one I was familiar with and viewed as old-school. I stressed out right away: "No way, we're not doing that," I said. "I don't want to use that tool; it's not good enough to meet our needs." My coworker took a different approach. She listened to me vent, went back to our IT contact, and asked him to show her the proposed solution. After a few more exchanges, she sent me an email outlining why IT's proposal actually worked in our favor.

I felt humbled, for a lot of reasons. One, she clearly took the time to be curious and get more information rather than shutting down right away, like I did. Two, she didn't view herself as the person who knew best; she stayed open to other perspectives and possibilities. And three, the entire situation reminded me to pay close attention to the moments when I immediately launch onto the warpath, because that's usually when I need to take a step back, cool off, and see what I'm missing.

If there's one thing I'm sure about, it's that life will give you plenty of lemons to make lemonade out of—trust me. So look for those moments of conflict when you or someone else gets all bent out of shape, and try to react with curiosity more than anything.

CHALLENGE #9:
Listen to Your Gut

Before I met my husband, I was engaged twice—and broke it off both times. One relationship should've simply ended years prior, despite good intentions; the other evolved into an emotionally abusive situation that proved tricky to escape. People usually stare at me openmouthed when they learn these stories, since broken engagements tend to be juicy tales of he said/she said drama. My experiences certainly involved their fair share of dramatic moments, for better or for worse, but they also taught me one central skill: how to listen to my gut.

Listening to your gut sounds simple, but it's more complicated in real life. You have to learn how to tune in to your intuition, trust your instincts, and navigate a whole host of thoughts and emotions that may or may not be accurate—and your gut might be in direct contrast with long-held narratives, what other people think and believe, or what seems to be logical. That's why it's worth practicing, so in this challenge we'll talk about some ways you can learn to associate trust with certain words, put habits into place that help you actually hear what your gut is "saying," and confidently follow through on a gut-based decision.

THINK ABOUT SOMEONE YOU TRUST AND HOW THAT TRUST MAKES YOU FEEL

Part of the work around listening to your gut involves understanding what trust feels like—with yourself or with someone else. From the first day I met my husband, I trusted him wholeheartedly, which is something I didn't experience in any of my previous relationships. I felt a sense of ease and belonging that I couldn't quite articulate; I didn't have to pretend or impress or perform. It wasn't love at first sight, but he felt like home.

There's no formula that works for everyone, but the more you identify people and situations that *do* bring forth this sense of "mmm, yes," the more you can practice tuning in to those types of feelings. And *that* means you'll be better equipped to notice when your gut instinct feels off, because it'll be distinctive.

Today think about a specific person you trust and find trustworthy, and write down a list of words you associate with that person in terms of how being around him makes you feel.

TRY THIS

Distinguish between how it feels when you trust someone and how it feels when you don't. Find a piece of paper and fold it in half. On one side, list all the ways your heart, mind, and body respond when you're around someone you trust. This might include words and phrases like the following: *calm, at ease, peaceful, happy, full of clarity.* On the opposite side, write down how it feels when you don't trust a person or situation—maybe words like *anxious, restless, lethargic, uncertain,* and *sick* come to mind. Use this piece of paper when you need a quick "gut check."

GIVE YOURSELF SPACE

I used to assume a gut feeling equaled instantaneous action: you have a deep-seated physical or emotional reaction to a situation or person, and then boom, you make a choice, make a move, make a decision accordingly. I've learned, though, it's better to give myself a bit of gap time in between a gut feeling and any resulting action—because that's how you avoid confusing a gut feeling with an emotional response in general. You know how some people will suggest getting a good night's sleep before a tough conversation? Same thing. With any decision that requires tuning in to your intuition when you need to hear and pay attention to your gut, give yourself some space. Whether you take a break, go for a short walk, or wait a couple of hours, gut feelings don't go anywhere with a little time; they only intensify, which is helpful in the long run.

Giving yourself space also helps you differentiate between fear and your true intuition. If you find yourself worrying about failure or thinking about being scared, you might be simply dealing with a risk regarding a choice about something that's different or new in your life, which is completely normal. On the other hand, your intuition may be harder to describe; you might just have a "feeling" that's a little off or taking shape in a pattern or direction out of the ordinary. That's your cue to investigate further, which is what taking space is all about.

FOLLOW THROUGH ON A GUT-BASED DECISION

Now for the tricky part: let's say you're dealing with a person or plan of action or project. You listen to your gut, and you have a good idea of what to do next—except that move doesn't really match what other people say you should do, what you originally thought you would do, what society says you should do, and so on. You feel stuck and start arguing with yourself, defending different choices you could make or convincing yourself one path is the correct one. Doubt creeps in, and all of a sudden you're back to square one, trying to figure out if you really had a gut feeling about something or not. Maybe you are dealing with a minor suspicion, or a full-blown sense of "This isn't right" or "Yes, I need to do this." Either way it can be hard to take steps based on a feeling alone.

This crossroad comes back to trust. When you're able to trust yourself, you're more in tune with your own intuition and can use it as a guiding force to follow through on decisions. Listening to your gut, or your intuition, is really an act of self-confidence: you believe you are doing the right thing, even if it looks different than what you anticipated or comes out of nowhere. You may not always get it right, and no outcome is guaranteed, but trusting a gut feeling is your best bet. Think of your intuition like a tool: the more you practice using it, the sharper your skills will become.

CHALLENGE #10:
Don't Lose Yourself

You ever notice how some dogs look like their owners? Sadahiko Nakajima, a psychologist who studies the resemblance between dogs and owners, says it's due to something called the "exposure effect": we prefer what feels familiar, so people tend to choose pets that look similar to them. This happens in other relationships too—if you've been with someone for a long time, a romantic partner or a friend, then occasionally you start to morph into each other, like an amalgam of personality. It can be sweet and reassuring, the sense of a collective "we" based on a constellation of years of experiences, but it can also backfire when you forget how to be your own person with individual needs, wants, desires, likes, fears, and goals.

My husband and I love spending time together, and I view him as one of the easiest people in my life to be around, all things considered. That doesn't mean I want to hang out with him 24/7, though, and when we start to be a little too attached at the hip, our relationship actually suffers. Having our respective hobbies and interests, weekend trips apart, favorite shows, and so on keeps life interesting. The same is true for many of my friends—it's cool to share an appreciation for iced coffee and travel and literature, but I also value learning from each friend based on our many differences.

This challenge either will help you carve out your own identity, if it's gotten a bit lost in the shuffle of your relationships, or will remind you of the benefits of preserving your own singular self.

NAME ONE THING YOU'RE INTERESTED IN AND MAKE TIME FOR IT

Every time I come across a bookstore—whether it's a major chain selling coffee and blockbusters, an independently owned storefront tucked away on a street corner, or a local shop offering stacks of dusty used books—my impulse is to stroll through. It makes me happy to walk down each aisle, pick up and hold each text, and see if I can find a hidden gem to bring home. I can easily spend an hour or two in a bookstore just sauntering around, and I can even leave without buying anything but still feeling relaxed and content. For me, it's not about buying a book; it's more of a pure luxury to simply walk around and look and think without being rushed.

Having this luxurious amount of time to stroll around and relax is a rare occasion as a working mama of two. Still, even thinking about doing this activity makes me feel happy inside, and if I'm having a shitty day, it's one of my go-to moves for refilling my own cup.

Despite my love of bookstore strolls, I don't actually stop by a bookstore that often. I have to remind myself once in a while to slow down and do the things I love to do, for no other reason than that they are enjoyable. My husband has his own set of things. And we don't need to do any of these activities together to enjoy them, because there's something fun about coming back to each other from these moments to share insights and stories.

Name one thing you love to do, but rarely do. It can be anything, but it has to be something you genuinely enjoy doing for no other reason than you think it's cool or fun or interesting. Now make time for that something just for the pure enjoyment of it.

TRY SOMETHING UNCOMFORTABLE

We all like to be comfortable, especially in our relationships with friends, partners, and family members. Sometimes it's more work to do something different or against the norm, and change and the unknown can be scary concepts. Yet letting yourself be lulled into a pattern of always doing what the people in your life want to do, because it is easier, will eventually take a toll on your identity and sense of self. It'll also get a little boring, no matter how much of a "creature of habit" you are! For example, my husband and I typically go to the same restaurants and bars, or do the same activities around town, whenever we sneak away for a date night. We love our norms and routines, but one year we decided we had to switch it up. We decided to do a monthly date...with one catch: the other person had to plan it completely on their own, and the person who wasn't planning it had to be game for anything. Our first outing? Ice skating outside—something I would never choose. Still, we had a blast, and the experience reminded me to try uncomfortable things once in a while.

The same is true for you as an individual. Sure, it's nice to have a buddy when you're dying to try that new lunch spot or travel across the country, but you can also venture out on your own, even if it makes you a little apprehensive or nervous. Try something new that piques your interest, even if it doesn't appeal to anyone else in your circle. Most of all, don't let a fear over conflict or approval get in the way of you actually doing what makes you happy.

DON'T RELY ON YOUR PARTNER TO COMPLETE YOU

"You...complete me." The minute Tom Cruise uttered these words in the movie *Jerry Maguire*, relationship experts everywhere probably cringed. I'm half joking. But seriously, other people are not ultimately responsible for your sense of wholeness, and it's dangerous to look to the relationships in your life to serve that purpose. The people you love can absolutely shape and guide you toward a feeling of being complete, but at the end of the day, your wholeness is up to *you*, and no relationship can meet every single need or desire you might have ever had. That's part of the work around not losing yourself—when you stay connected to your own sense of self, you can flourish but also make space for how you may want to grow and change throughout different chapters of your life.

Focus on what makes you *you*, outside of the context of any relationship.

TRY THIS

When you think about what "completes" you, what comes to mind? Write it down. Now go back and see how many things on your list are related to other people. Cross them off, and try again. What gives you a sense of love and purpose? How can you complete yourself and let other people serve as the cherry on top?

Part 4

Finance

I didn't grow up in a family with a ton of money, but we had enough. We also didn't talk about finances very much, which I later realized influenced my entire attitude around this topic: as a conversation to be avoided unless absolutely necessary. As a young adult, I fell squarely into a circular camp of naiveté: I didn't think I knew "enough" (whatever that means) about finances, which made me feel stupid, so I avoided learning more—until I dug myself into a hole of credit card and student loan debt. For a long time, paying off debt felt too impossible, too long of a road. Any amount I could technically repurpose toward debt seemed like a drop in the bucket, but eventually the desire to develop better money smarts won out.

Money, whether you have a little or plenty or not enough, evokes emotion, and your financial skills often depend on a constellation of experiences: how you were raised, how your parents handled money, the reality of your paycheck over the years, the amount of debt you have or lack thereof, job security, and more. In this part we'll talk about how you can do the same: rid yourself of debt, actually build an emergency fund, donate on a budget, save for retirement, know exactly where your money goes, plan for birthdays and special occasions, and live based on your means. After all, money is power—but more than that, it's freedom.

CHALLENGE #1:
Pay Off a Debt

When I moved to Chicago in 2008, I had zero credit card debt. Four years later I left with $10,000. You might be thinking, *Holy irresponsibility!* (Yup.) Or maybe you're frantically checking your own credit card statement, feeling All the Bad Feelings. (Been there.) Either way, when this happened to me, I did not immediately create a budget or cut up my cards or tell a friend or seek money management advice...or consider my money habits or feelings in general. I just avoided the problem and assumed that one day I'd be able to pay off this debt.

And I did, eventually—but not because I buried my head in the sand until my fairy godmother waved her wand and cleared my balance. Chipping away at this debt took several years of hard work based on hundreds of tiny, proactive financial decisions. I didn't win the lottery or get a massive raise at work or come into family money; I slogged through it, and most of the time it sucked. Have you ever heard that phrase "Nothing tastes as good as skinny feels"? For me, it was more like "No purchase feels as good as seeing a zero balance."

DON'T SPEND A DIME TODAY

Okay, maybe this won't exactly be *easy*, but it is definitely the least painful way to glance at your spending habits and see if there are ways you could possibly make adjustments. Your challenge? Don't spend any money for one day, outside of any necessary bills, prescheduled payments, or absolute necessities. Every time you think about buying something or spending money, ask yourself if it could wait until tomorrow. Again, there's no need to deprive yourself of anything you need, but see where you could cut it down to the bare minimum.

Then track what you *would've* spent. For example, I do a No Spend Day at least once a month (if not more), and one of my recent lists looked like this: coffee ($2), sandals for an upcoming vacation ($50), lunch ($10), donation to a coworker's baby shower ($10), fresh tomatoes for a dinner recipe ($5), diapers ($25). Instead I brought coffee from home, paused on the sandals until I have a discount code to use next month for my birthday, scraped together leftovers in a brown bag, decided to donate to the shower on my next payday since I technically have time to wait, made the recipe using canned tomatoes out of my pantry at home, and used up remaining diapers at home before picking more up. And then I put an additional $102 toward my student loan bill, just like that. Of course, that scenario is based on the privilege of having a "spare" $102 to spend, but in my head, if I already intended to spend that sum on all these other little "wants," then I might as well put it toward debt.

Another option is to avoid spending extra money, but instead pick a reasonably small amount that you could put toward one debt on that same day; it can be as little as $5. Don't stress about the amount—anything is better than nothing, and taking action will make you feel somewhat virtuous.

CUT OUT ALL THE EXTRAS

Learning how to live within your means is vital for financial peace of mind, so for this challenge you'll essentially dare yourself to see how much money you could save in a week if you really tried. It may feel a little self-sacrificing, but it's short-term, so you can do it. Cut out every single extra purchase for seven days, or give yourself a set amount to put toward debt for seven days.

At the end of the week, note where you are, and use that money to pay off some debt. Since this time frame of a week is slightly longer, you may want to introduce the reward element—for example, if you save $100 this week, you can spend $10 on yourself.

TARGET ONE DISTINCT AMOUNT OF DEBT

With a challenge like this, first decide what you're trying to accomplish. Do you want to pay off $300 of credit card debt? Reduce your car loan by $1,000? Pay down an extra $50 on tuition for your kid? Whatever you pick, make it meaningful and specific. I chose a monthly goal: "I want to pay off half of this $500 loan. How can I make this happen?"

Naturally that's the million-dollar question. You can be aggressive or take a slower approach, depending on your goals, money habits, financial situation, and personality type. I've done both—I've taken every extra cent in a certain month and put it toward debt, and I've reworked my monthly budget to put an extra $25 toward debt in full. In the end it's a numbers game that's entirely up to you, but find traction. Get the ball rolling so you feel like your debt is not insurmountable (even if that feeling is temporary!), and you can see tangible before and after numbers.

Find five major spending habits and focus on those: dining out, sticking to a grocery store list, avoiding impromptu purchases, deleting sale emails. Kinda dull and obvious, but that's intentional—the behaviors you need to change in order to save money, so you can pay off debt, are probably fairly obvious once you look around. It's just a matter of being willing to put in the work and hold yourself accountable—but when it comes to debt, you've gotta start somewhere.

TRY THIS

Think about a financial debt you'd like to pay off, and for the next thirty days, redirect all your "extra" money to additional payments. Take one of two approaches: every time you spend money on something that isn't essential, immediately put that same amount toward your debt. Or set all those amounts of money off to the side in a savings account, then at the end of the month, put a large lump sum toward your debt.

CHALLENGE #2:
Build an Emergency Fund

I've always been told that you need to have three to six months of living expenses in an emergency fund. That's what "they" say, anyway. Here's what I want to know: who are "they," and what world are they living in? Because in my experience, saving for an emergency is like watching your sink leak: drip, drip, drip. It can slowly add up to a puddle, and then a small dish, and maybe even a stockpot, but man, it takes a long time. Also, what constitutes living expenses—rent, electricity, water, and food? What about daycare costs? A car accident? A surprise hospital bill? A DIY home project that ends up being much more expensive than anticipated? Finally, let's say you do build up some sort of emergency fund: do you ever touch it?

Clearly I have a lot of questions, mostly because I love the security blanket an emergency fund can provide. But if you're anything like me, you might also find it difficult to put a bunch of money in one spot, "just in case," and stare at it every time you open your checking account. These challenges will help you find a good middle ground, where you've got a line of defense but you're also not completely panicking about the amount you've set aside.

DECIDE WHY AN EMERGENCY FUND MATTERS TO YOU

After I graduated from college, I kept about $500 in my savings account. I thought that was pretty decent, considering I held a fairly low-paying communications job, lived in a big city, had health insurance, and didn't necessarily anticipate a lot of big expenses. For a while that was fine. Until I needed to move out of an apartment unexpectedly due to a breakup. And then another apartment, because I couldn't make rent. Then my car got towed three times in six months. I had no funds to help me handle those situations, so I relied on my parents, my grandparents, and my trusty credit card to pay for breaking a lease, moving costs, and towing recovery. I'm beyond grateful that I had such support from family members and access to credit—not everyone has backup options like that—but it was terrible. It also made me realize things were bound to happen outside of my direct control, and I ultimately wanted to feel empowered to handle them from a financial perspective without relying on other people or increasing the balance on my credit card.

That's why an emergency fund matters to me: it's a sense of security. For you, it may be a different reason: cash set aside for a true emergency (like a car accident), a fund that can support you in a particular situation (like if you lose your job), or simply money in the bank in case you need to make a major purchase (like buying a new refrigerator). When you know why you want to set some dollars aside, it becomes easier to take the steps to do it. So take some time today and write down a few reasons why having money set aside is important to you.

AUTOMATE YOUR SAVINGS

When my husband and I were first dating, a hailstorm caused serious damage to our cars. In response I panicked; he merely sighed and looked up his insurance information. We then had a conversation that went like this.

Me: "Great. This is going to be expensive to fix."

Him: "Yeah, what's your deductible?"

Me: "Um..."

Him: "You don't know what your car insurance deductible is?"

Me: "No? I'm pretty sure I just picked the one with the lowest monthly payment."

Him: "Gotcha. Well, I automatically transfer money every week so I have a couple thousand set aside for when stuff like this happens."

It was a light-bulb moment for me: if I proactively set aside money for situations like this, I wouldn't have to completely stress out when they happened, because I would know that I could financially handle the expense. Now I have an automatic transfer set up to move money to savings accounts for various known expenses, like home repair and car maintenance. I never have to think about it, aside from when I want to adjust the amount or see where I am.

Automate your own savings. Instead of saving whatever amount of money is left over at the end of each paycheck, think of it as automatically paying yourself *first*. It's like you never even had the money to begin with, which is a good thing—it'll be easier to avoid the temptation of spending it! First, decide how much money you'd like to set aside; ideally it's as much as you can manage per your budget, but even $10 a week functions as a great starting point. Then talk with your bank, credit union, or financial institution to figure out what types of savings accounts are available, and how you can avoid balance requirements or monthly fees. You can also set up direct deposit with many employers and fill out paperwork to transfer part of your paycheck to a specific bank account. It is less complicated than you think!

SET A SAVINGS GOAL

How much money would you like to save in an ideal world? If your answer is "lots," I feel you, but also, let's get more specific. Your emergency fund is just one piece of the pie, and having different accounts can be a great way to save for various needs. I've found it also helps to identify an initial goal, even if it seems completely out of reach. A couple of years ago, my husband and decided to try to save $10,000. Did we have that kind of money lying around? No. Did we know if we could save that much? Not exactly. Did it seem like a crazy goal? Yes, to me. But I kept it in my mind as something to reach toward with our savings habits. We set up an automatic savings plan to set aside $100 per week, and after two years of aggressively saving, we finally hit the mark. That slow-and-steady approach eventually became a nonnegotiable habit; even in months with a tighter budget, we did our best to stick to it, no matter what. And it worked.

Pick a savings goal, whether that's just for an emergency or as a whole. Your goal can be significantly smaller or larger than mine was. No matter the actual number, use your weekly saving strategy to figure out how long it'll take to save that amount of money.

TRY THIS

Set a savings goal in terms of how much money you'd like to save within the year. Be realistic—yes, of course more is better, but what's a target you can potentially reach? Now work backward. Divide that sum of money by twelve months. That's your monthly target. Divide *that* by four, and you've got a weekly amount to aim to save. Again, a little goes a long way: $25 a week can add up to more than $1,000!

CHALLENGE #3:

Donate on a Budget

I once worked for a large urban church in downtown Chicago, which hosted a fancy fund-raiser every year. At a certain point in the evening, the host invited the crowd to raise a wooden paddle in a show of open-ended giving: Who wants to donate $500? What about $1,500? Any takers for $5,000? My twenty-two-year-old self wondered if I'd ever be in a financial position to write that kind of check, and I viewed my paltry $25 a year donation as insignificant in comparison.

But that's all I could afford on a shoestring budget, and I know lots of other people are in the same boat. I felt self-conscious about giving only a little bit of money here and there; however, there's no reason to be embarrassed. A donation is a donation, regardless of the amount. Philanthropy is less about how *much* you give to a cause or organization, and more about your willingness to be consistent, informed, and active, whether you choose to donate your time or money or both. You don't have to wait until you're a millionaire before you decide to give back, and donating small amounts of money is entirely possible—and worthwhile—without going broke.

THINK ABOUT WHAT YOU STAND FOR AND FIND A CAUSE THAT COINCIDES WITH IT

I went to a Catholic school growing up, where every student had to earn two hundred service hours in order to graduate. Though it wasn't hard for me to meet the requirement, it mostly felt like one big "should." As a result, when I entered my twenties, I automatically looked for ways to serve my community, not from a place of intention but one of obligation. Donating and volunteering were things that "good" people did, so I "should" do them. Eventually I realized that having a sense of true purpose around a particular cause would probably make the entire effort way more fulfilling. I did a little soul-searching and discovered I cared deeply about supporting public art, young writers, and technology for at-risk communities. I joined the young professionals' board of my local art center and set up a recurring donation to two nonprofits, one that provided spoken word poetry workshops to teenagers and another that focused on coding classes for refugee students.

What specific causes matter to you? Which industries or fields do you have access to, and how can you make a difference? What's your motivation for donating your time or money? Perhaps an answer comes to mind right away, which is great. If it doesn't, spend a little time contemplating. Your *why* matters quite a bit. You can't be all things to all people, and you probably don't have unlimited time or money to devote, so consider how you can align your pocketbook or calendar to your sense of purpose. Pick an organization or causes that you feel strongly about, and come up with a few reasons as to why they matter to you.

DONATE TIME OR MONEY TO YOUR CAUSE

Early on, when I couldn't really afford to donate regularly, I would at least try to devote an hour of my time once in a while to a local charity or nonprofit. I figured that was better than nothing: I didn't necessarily have the cash to spend, but I could volunteer an hour on the weekend or after work. I also liked the fact that by showing up in person, I could see first-hand how an organization worked as well as who potentially benefited. On the flip side, when I finally reached a point in my career where I could allocate money to different causes, I also appreciated the instantaneous feeling of "I'm helping" that came with hitting the donate button or writing a check.

Either way, within a week I'm guessing you could do one or the other. Those organizations that came to mind in the easy exercise? Look 'em up. How can you help? Do you have an hour or thirty minutes to spare? Five or ten bucks? Don't overthink it; just do it.

TRY THIS

Pick one cause or organization that's close to your heart, and show your support in the next week. Sign up to volunteer, budget for a monthly or annual donation, attend an event to learn more, or simply give the group a call and say, "I want to help. What can I do?"

SHOW UP REGULARLY FOR YOUR CAUSE

I'm one of those people who has a tendency to donate the second someone pulls on my heartstrings. Give me a national or local crisis, and I'm there with my credit card out, ready to offer up what I can. I'm also really good at showing up when it's all preplanned, like an annual volunteer opportunity with friends or coworkers. But over the past two years, I started noticing a difference between operating from reactive mode—someone needs help! I can help!—and making an active, deliberate choice to regularly support the causes I cared about. I kept saying that certain organizations mattered to me, but I didn't really do anything to show up for them until prompted, and only once in a while. And I started wondering if maybe I needed to do a bit more of the latter. I wanted to, for lack of a better phrase, put my money where my mouth was.

Because there's something powerful about regularly showing up. It requires sacrifice, planning, and going outside of your comfort zone. Even though philanthropy isn't about you necessarily, if you're not committed to showing up, it's harder to feel like your money and your time will actually make a difference. Over the course of, say, a month, how could you do this? Does it mean a bigger donation based on your budget? Volunteering a couple of times? Both? It's totally up to you, but notice what changes when you adopt an attitude of stepping up more than you usually do.

CHALLENGE #4:
Look at Your Paycheck

Like everybody else, I love getting paid—but most of the time, I immediately glance at the number going into my bank account for reassurance and move right along. I don't exactly dissect the details; I assume everything is correct even though I don't *totally* know where all my money goes. Isn't that weird, though? I work hard for that paycheck, as I imagine you work hard for yours, so it makes sense to spend five minutes every other week or every month confirming the accuracy. Errors happen *all* the time, and while we'd probably both like to assume our human resources or payroll or contracting departments are studiously reviewing each paycheck that goes out the door, the reality is that they're human and mistakes are bound to happen eventually. In this challenge we'll talk about why you need to go over any and all paychecks with a fine-tooth comb, and how to make sure you understand what's going in and out of your accounts.

FIND AND REVIEW YOUR MOST RECENT PAYCHECK(S)

Think for a second: where *is* your paycheck? Online? In an envelope somewhere on a desk? Does it get mailed to your house every two weeks or show up through some sort of electronic system? If you freelance or maintain a side hustle, do you have all your receipts or checks in one place that indicate pay received? Now's the time to make sure. From there, go through your paycheck(s) line by line, and make a note of the terms you don't understand or the dollar amounts that seem confusing.

I'm a recovering money-averse person, so it takes some mental fortitude to look at a paycheck and ensure that I understand all the terms listed. In my brain the initial reaction is more like "Say whaaaa," with an itch to put it away and again assume all is well; I have to kind of force myself to stay the course for a little education. Here are some of the terms you'll likely see: total gross pay, total net pay, hours worked, paid time off, and deductions like tax withholdings and benefits. Within those last two categories, money is usually withheld for things like Social Security, Medicare, federal tax, state tax, city tax, retirement, medical insurance, dental insurance, vision insurance, life or disability insurance, flex spending, and much more. Why does all of this matter? Well, let's say you're getting paid a salary of $50,000. The hard truth is that you're not bringing that entire sum home, and it's important to understand not only where all of your money goes, but also why.

LOOK AT A FULL MONTH'S PAYCHECKS TO MAKE SURE EVERYTHING IS ACCURATE

Just the other month I received a direct deposit for a couple of articles I had written, and as I briefly looked it over, I realized I had been shortchanged about $200. I went back through my own invoicing system to confirm, and sure enough, the client was wrong. I emailed my contact to explain, sent over a copy of the invoice I had originally sent, and within about a business day, she replied with "Oh, sorry! We'll get that corrected." Which wouldn't have happened if I hadn't been closely paying attention. Although you might assume it's the responsibility of a company to pay you correctly (and it should, of course), that's only an expectation on your part—you need to validate too.

Take a little time to go through a full month's pay. Look at hours worked or your salary. See if your deductions were handled properly, both company-paid ones as well as the benefits you're responsible for. If you've made any changes recently, like a new address, direct deposit updates, a change in insurance or other benefits, or a 401(k) contribution adjustment, then you'll want to review all of that. If any details are wrong, reach out to get it corrected as soon as possible.

THINK ABOUT YOUR LONG-TERM FINANCIAL GOALS

The previous challenge might trigger you to think about your long-term career or financial goals. By *long-term*, I mean in the next five years or longer, versus shorter-term goals that can be achieved in the next year or so. Your income empowers you to move toward both types of goals, but there's a big difference between saving $50 per paycheck to put toward a vacation and doing so for a down payment on a house. For instance, a recent short-term goal involved saving for the hospital bill related to the birth of our second child. We knew how much we'd need to save and when we'd need the money. At the same time, I have a long-term financial goal to pay off my student loans.

Every time you look at your paycheck, think about what you're trying to do and how you can make smart fiscal decisions to succeed. Do you want to contribute more toward your retirement so you can retire early? Receive different benefits for more coverage or less money taken out per month? Would you like to work toward a higher salary, explore a promotion, or put your hat in the ring for a higher-paying job elsewhere? Start a side hustle for a secondary income stream? Make six figures upon reaching a particular age? When you know the structure of your pay in full, it positions you to take more steps toward financial independence.

TRY THIS

Have you heard of S.M.A.R.T. goals? This strategy emphasizes particular characteristics of goal-setting for better results; the best goals are supposedly specific, measurable, achievable, realistic, and time-bound. Let's say you'd love to vacation more frequently. For your best chance at reaching that goal, it needs to be specific (vacation where?), measurable (how much will it cost?), achievable (what might you do to budget accordingly?), realistic (what sorts of milestones do you need to keep your savings on track?), and time-bound (how soon do you want to go on that first vacation?). After you take a look at your paycheck, set a financial goal for ten years down the road, and make it S.M.A.R.T.

CHALLENGE #5:
Take a Cash-Only Approach

I'll be honest—personally this particular challenge is extremely difficult for me whenever I give it a try. I love the ease of using my debit card, hate the process of taking out cash, and dislike carrying around a bunch of singles and change. Maybe it's generational. My dad is old-school; he always has a little bit of cash on him, "just in case," and I understand the rationale for having some dollar bills in case you run into a cash-only situation. Despite my resistance, I also recognize cash works as a crystal clear way to be mindful of your spending. What you see is what you get, and when you don't have any more, you're S.O.L. Utilizing a cash-only strategy for a day, a week, and a month opens your eyes to how you budget, whether you're budgeting effectively, and exactly how you spend money. It also helps you feel a sense of ownership over the money you've earned and realize its value. Give it a try.

USE ONLY CASH TODAY

This exercise is pretty straightforward. Use only cash for whenever you need to spend money today, excluding any usual bills or expenses that might be prescheduled or handled automatically. Stop at the ATM first thing in the morning and then use only that cash today. It'll be like a gut check: either you won't spend a dime for a day, or you'll be more like me and keep reaching for your card out of habit as you watch your cash dwindle, uh, rather quickly. Neither reaction is wrong, but both will make you think twice about your spending habits. I'll venture to guess that you will be shocked at how quickly your cash goes, and it will hopefully force you to look at your spending habits and adjust them so you can stretch your money out to last the whole day. What happens if you run out of cash before the day is over? Use it as a kind of a test to see if you can make it through the rest of the day without spending any more money.

USE ONLY CASH FOR A WEEK

This obviously takes the previous exercise up a notch. Again, excluding your major expenses (like rent and utilities and such), take out a sum of money at the beginning of the week and use that cash whenever you need to pay for something. For example, if I take out $100 on a Sunday, then my goal is to use that amount of money for every single purchase that's not already planned or absolutely necessary. My Monday morning pick-me-up of a cold brew coffee and a cranberry scone? $7. Flowers for a friend as a thank-you present for helping me out last month with a photo shoot? $10. Lunch with coworkers? $12. Gas? $50. Aaaaand there goes the $100, just like that.

You might be a little shocked at how quickly your cash can disappear within a given week—but experts say people are more likely to overspend, or spend more freely, using a credit card versus cash, so maybe it's not that surprising at all. The benefit of using only cash in a week is that you start to limit your discretionary spending or at least notice how your habits add up, cost-wise, in order to potentially make different decisions. My husband and I are comfortable in a financial sense, but I certainly don't need or want to blow $100 in a week like it's NBD. Which means I can drink coffee at home before work, skip the scone, and bring my lunch in order to prioritize spending that is more important to me.

TRY THIS

Based on your budget, think through where you can easily switch to cash only. For example, you probably can't pay your rent with cash, but things like clothing, groceries, snacks, and meals out are fair game. Set aside a certain amount of cash for these areas, and then for the next week, avoid using a debit or credit card for any related purchases.

USE ONLY CASH FOR A THIRTY-DAY PERIOD

DIFFICULTY LEVEL:

HARD

Take the lessons you've learned, for better or worse, from the previous two exercises, and apply them toward a thirty-day period of time. Using cash for an entire month is going to require discipline, particularly if you're used to swiping your card for every little thing. It will also force you to consider the repercussions of each purchase from a need versus want standpoint: if you eat leftover pasta in your fridge for dinner instead of buying Chipotle, then you have more money for the next day, and the next—so what's more important to you? You also might technically run out of money in the month, and it'll be your choice to either take more money out (hey, I'm not judging you) or survive in a no-spend land for the remainder of the thirty days.

That's why this type of challenge is so effective: cards are convenient, but the downside is that purchases don't exactly feel "real," and it's very easy to spend your money on things that aren't necessary in a given moment, or things that cost a bit more than you would've planned. You can look at your bank statement later on, but by that point the damage is already done. With cash you don't have that luxury, which means you have to be pretty diligent about the way you spend and show restraint. It might also directly impact the way you socialize, considering most of us spend money (a lot of it!) hanging out with friends and family members— date nights, weekend trips, seeing a new play, happy hour, grabbing a taxi—so plan on giving the people you usually spend time with a heads-up that your month may look a little different than normal. Aka, you'll need to find cheaper or free options.

Keep in mind that the point of cash-only exercises isn't to live an all-cash lifestyle (unless you want to, but it's probably fairly unrealistic). It's to help get your spending back on track and better align your budget to your actual spending habits or lifestyle.

Experiment with Delayed Gratification

When I was growing up, my mom's mantra was "Let's wait to see if it goes on sale." She is a clearance queen, in the best way possible—that woman can find a deal like no other, whether she's negotiating a *Craigslist* item, browsing her local TJ Maxx, or rapidly flipping through the sale rack at her favorite department store. I still vividly remember shopping for high school dances. Most of the girls I knew had parents who spent upward of $250 at the minimum on a dress, hair, and makeup. My mom's budget was $50, no negotiation, but somehow we always found the coolest, most unique dresses. While I did have moments of wishing I could be like everyone else in my class, I recognized, even back then, how my mom's frugality was not only smart but also had no bearing on an end result. We could find the same full-price, name-brand items at a lower cost, and look good doing it—just at a later point than what was deemed popular.

Delayed gratification is a skill, albeit a rusty one for some people. With this challenge focus on the difference between purchases that actually add value to your life and ones you make out of habit or a self-determined "want" disguised as a "need." Waiting might make you feel a little stressed or itchy to have the item in question, but keep telling yourself that if it's meant to be, it'll work out, and you'll likely save money in the process.

USE THE "WANT OR NEED?" QUESTION BEFORE SPENDING MONEY

The other weekend I picked up some fresh tomatoes at the farmers' market. The next day I thought about going to the store to buy a baguette and mozzarella so we could make bruschetta, because it sounded good. Never mind that we had plenty of food we could make at home. My mind just thought: *Bruschetta sounds delicious; let's go buy stuff to make that.* And too often that's exactly what we do. A big deal? No. My husband and I cook a lot at home, which definitely saves us money in the long run, except when we start to make specific meals on a daily basis based on whatever we're craving. When we do that every day, those small extras add up. And though we certainly need to eat dinner, it doesn't have to be an exact meal based on a whim.

For this challenge, pause before every purchase and ask yourself: "Do I need this or do I want this?" That's all. Don't worry about the answer—it's okay to have a mix of both, and it's even okay to realize, *Yikes, I succumb to a ton of wants.* Just take that moment before spending money to think: want or need? Then categorize mentally.

TRACK YOUR AMOUNT OF WANTS VERSUS NEEDS

Now it's time to take the previous challenge and make it more visual and tangible. For a whole week, ask yourself, "Want or need?" before every purchase, and then write it down somewhere—whether it was a want or a need, as well as how much you ended up spending—to create a money diary. Again, you don't have to actually change the way you spend (yet!); you're just paying close attention to how your spending shakes out and making note of it.

At the end of the week, tally up how many "wants" and "needs" you had and the resulting cost of each. (Try to be as "normal" with your financial habits as possible, since that'll give you the truest picture of where you are.) Now look at your list. How many "wants"did you indulge in this week, and how much extra money did they end up costing you? You might be surprised how much of your hard-earned cash you let go of on things you didn't necessarily need but just wanted to have in the moment. It can be eye-opening to see your purchases laid out like this. Also, be mindful of where you start rationalizing the difference between a want and a need. Do you really "need" that sweater, or are you just feeling the itch to spice up your wardrobe? Which purchases can wait, and which ones are seriously essential?

TRY THIS

Review your spending for the past six months, and categorize every purchase as "want" or "need." It's okay if you don't account for every single purchase; you're just looking to see which way your spending habits lean. Tally up each column to see how much you spent, per month, on each. From there, set a goal to reduce your "want" spending by 25 percent (or more!), and set a reminder on your calendar to repeat the exercise.

WAIT ON THE "WANTS"

Last year my mom and sisters and I were shopping in a cute boutique, where we stumbled across a pair of black mules. I loved the shoes, but the shop didn't have my size, so I asked the store owner to give me a call when she got them back in stock. I didn't hear from her for months, and every so often I'd look up the shoes at an online retailer, think about buying them, and shake my head at the full price. My mom's words kept coming back to haunt me, and I knew they'd probably go on sale eventually—or I could live without them. Besides, I didn't "need" these shoes in the least. But every time I saw someone wearing a pair of chic black mules, I thought about this one particular pair and how if I owned them, I'd wear them all the time. Then one day my mom called. "Remember those black shoes you wanted?" "Yeah," I said. "Did you ever buy them?" "No, I kept waiting for them to go on sale," I replied. "Well, I just found them at that same store, in your size, at 40 percent off." Sold. The funny thing is that I sort of knew that would happen eventually, because practicing delayed gratification usually pays off.

That example included a yearlong wait, but the sentiment rings true. So for one whole month, don't buy anything deemed as a "want," but put it on a mental or real list to purchase in the future. Whether it's a tote bag for work, a new pair of brown boots to replace the ones that fell apart last season, your favorite face lotion that's on the expensive side, a book you've been wanting to read, a plane ticket for an upcoming trip— acknowledge that you want these things and may eventually buy them, but wait at least thirty days before you do so. The payoff? When you *do* bite the bullet, it'll feel like a real treat, something you've earned.

Plan for the Expected

You thought I was going to say plan for the *unexpected*, right? Nope. I'm talking about all the life expenses that seem to come out of nowhere, but really aren't that surprising: Christmas presents, birthday gifts, a haircut, new tennis shoes, traveling to attend a wedding, pet grooming, gardening, babysitters, dry cleaning, and so on. Ideally you'd plan for these sorts of costs on a regular basis, but for many people, these costs function as forgotten expenses since they're not ongoing purchases and not obvious bills—and they can seriously blow your budget.

What you need to do instead is factor the expected into your spending. If you know you generally spend $500 on holiday gifts for family members, set up an automatic savings plan to separately prep for that all year so you're not dipping into money meant for other things or relying on a credit card. If you and your partner love to throw parties in the summertime, save money specifically for that so you're not caught off guard by the cost of cheese plates and bottles of wine. You probably already have a good sense of where, when, and how you tend to spend a little more than usual (ahem, Target) as well as expenses that crop up semi-regularly and annually. Plan for them. Worst case scenario, you end up having extra money left over at the end of the year.

PINPOINT YOUR BUDGET WEAKNESS

I used to tease my mother for always giving little gifts to friends and family members. As I've gotten older, though, I've realized that I'm the exact same way. I pride myself on giving thoughtful presents to the people I love, recognizing their peaks and valleys with some sort of tangible item or simply demonstrating my affection for them. Whether you got a promotion at work or you're having a tough day after your divorce, I'm always going to want to reach out in the form of a gift. The downside? It adds up! While I've gotten much better at this over the years, I still accidentally find myself buying $50 in "just because" cards at the store or overspending on behalf of other people. And even though this behavior is certainly nice, all these little costs also directly impact my ability to budget suitably and reach my own financial goals.

This is what is called a budget weakness, and most people have at least one. It's a behavior that prompts you to spend more money than necessary. It could be brand-name-only items at the grocery store. Skin care products when you already have a drawer full at home. Shoes on sale. Craft beer. Birthdays. (Note: you might have more than one weakness!)

If you hope to get your finances in any sort of line, then you need to pinpoint your budget weakness. It's that item or service or treat that you may try to avoid or lessen, but when push comes to shove, you throw your hands in the air and say, "Whatever, I'm buying this." It may take some soul-searching, or even reviewing credit card or bank statements, to pinpoint what your weakness is, but once you know what it is, you can better prepare for it. You need to know your (budget) enemy to fight it, after all.

Pinpoint your own personal budget weaknesses so you can look out for red flags and warning signs regarding when you're about to shell out some cash versus show some restraint.

MAKE A LIST TO AVOID OVERSPENDING ON REPLACEMENT ITEMS

I'll go to Target for, like, a toilet bowl brush and somehow walk out $200 poorer, which is clearly a luxury but also kind of a problem. It's not that I'm buying cute notebooks and all-natural granola bars, either—it's stuff like face wash, soap, toothpaste, paper towels. Riveting, I know. But I see those items and think, *Oh, I'm almost out of this at home, so I better get it now.*

The problem? Being "almost" out of something isn't the same as being actually out of it. I hate running out of necessary items. I also don't need five bottles of shampoo in my bathroom closet.

This unorganized shopping adds up in terms of budget and storage, so make a list of the things you are in critical need of running out of and then buy *only* those items. This conscious buying has another benefit too; you'll start to notice patterns in your usage and that will help you budget for planned future expenses. *I always run out of this size shampoo in four weeks, I always seem to need a pack of toilet paper every two weeks,* you get the idea.

Think through the items that will need to be replaced soon, and consider if you can wait until you're truly out of them or if you need to stock up accordingly. Then make a list and plan for those expenses instead of catching your budget off guard.

TRY THIS

Look around your home, and make a list of only the items you've run out of and need to replace *now*. Then go shopping, and buy only the items on your list. Sure, in theory this sounds like a basic task, but you will be surprised by how difficult it can be. If you get to the store and see an item that you don't absolutely need right now but think you will run out of soon, write it down on a separate list or as a note in your phone to add it to next month's shopping trip, but do not buy it if it is not on your list.

SAVE FOR ANNUAL COSTS THAT ALWAYS SNEAK UP ON YOU

DIFFICULTY LEVEL:

HARD

My family made two major budget shifts over the past couple of years. We set up two separate, specific savings accounts: one for car taxes and registration, and one for the holidays. On the car front, my husband was sick of getting the yearly bill to renew the registration for our two vehicles, and with the holidays, I hated the financial beating our bank account took every November and early December.

Here's what we did to be more prepared and intentional with our money: we took these two fixed and variable costs, divided them by twelve, and pulled money out of our checking account every single month for each. It worked; we now know not only how much money we have to play with when these situations arise but also where to pull that money from.

Think about your annual costs, like holidays, that you know are coming but that always seem to strain your budget. Then take the total cost of that expense (or an estimated cost based on the previous year's spending) and divide it down into more manageable payments. How you save these payments is up to you; you can set up a separate account at your bank or even simply pull the money together in a savings jar on your kitchen countertop. Then, when these expenses roll around, you won't be left feeling drained of cash and resentful.

CHALLENGE #8:

Cut Down Recurring Expenses

One life hack I've heard about from high-performing leaders and CEOs involves minimizing recurring obligations at work, such as attending weekly meetings—not because such meetings aren't important, but because every calendar item that requires a time commitment on a frequent basis adds up over time and eventually takes up all your time. The same is true for recurring expenses: it may seem like it's "just" ten or twenty bucks, but at some point those amounts of money add up to a bigger cost. Some fixed costs are unavoidable, like your mortgage or car payment or taxes, and others are actually fixed costs that could shift to variable, like your Netflix account, subscription boxes, parking fees, booze habits, and magazine purchases. Just because you regularly devote money to these items doesn't mean you have to, and so this challenge is all about cutting out such expenses within your budget.

NOTE ALL YOUR RECURRING EXPENSES

Nowadays there's a fee-based subscription or membership for almost everything: news publications, meal planning services, workout apps, web hosting, streaming shows, professional training videos, beauty and hygiene boxes or clubs, Internet, the gym, and much more. Most use a monthly model—you pay a certain amount, and you get something in return. Some of these can make your life way easier, some are just fluffy and fun, and others help you stay fit, educated, and connected. (This probably goes without saying, but the vast majority are also a total luxury, assuming you have extra cash to use in this way.)

The first step is to flat-out make a list of which ones you've registered for and how much each is actually costing you. You may see a few you totally forgot about or haven't even used in the past couple of months, or there may be some on your list that originally started as a free trial but now incur a charge. Also, pay attention to any programs or services that essentially offer the same thing, like Netflix and Hulu or Spotify and Apple Music. You don't have to do anything about these expenses quite yet; simply outline what they are and make sure you know exactly what's hitting your bank account.

ASSESS HOW OFTEN YOU USE THESE SERVICES OR PROGRAMS

I once signed up for a meal delivery subscription pre-children, and my husband and I had a blast cooking different, unique meals and switching up our dinnertime game. Then we had kids, and while I know plenty of parents who thrive with these types of services, it just didn't work for us. When we received a box of meals, we mostly reacted with "Ugh, now we have to make this, and we had to pay for it." So we stopped using it—and after, oh, six months of logging into the website to cancel another week of meals before getting charged, I finally asked myself, "Why don't I just cancel the subscription itself?" Duh. Another example: we were paying about eight bucks a month for a certain streaming service. At one juncture in time, I watched several different shows and movies through the platform, so it got a lot of use, but for some reason, I stopped. When I kept seeing the charge appear on my credit card, I again, finally, asked myself: "Why am I paying for this when I don't use it to watch anything?" Duh times two.

Go back to that list you made in the easy challenge, and next to every single item, figure out the last time you used each one. If it's not in the past month, flag it. If it's a situation where you constantly have to log in to push back use so you don't get charged, flag it. If you straight up can't remember or you're, like, "What is this again?" flag it.

REDUCE AS MANY RECURRING EXPENSES AS POSSIBLE

Take your flagged list from the medium challenge and parcel out which recurring expenses you'd like to keep—meaning that the cost fits your budget and you actively use whatever it is for a specific purpose—and which ones you flagged. Take the questionable ones and think through whether or not you'd like to keep them, or if you can find a way to bring the price down. For example, maybe you can pause the service for six months to reevaluate down the road (in other words, see if you even miss it), or you can call a customer service representative and ask for a discount, or you can share certain services with friends or family members to make it cheaper for everyone involved. Push yourself to make the list of what remains as short as possible, and notice if you're using a lot of pushy reasoning with yourself—like "But my dog, Dolly, loves her box of treats every month..." I mean, if that's important to you, great! Just be real. Not every subscription or monthly membership is a bad thing, but all cost money. If you were to cancel the vast majority and put those funds elsewhere, you could probably go sit on a beach with a fancy umbrella drink. I'm just saying.

TRY THIS

Look at your budget and spending habits, and for the next three months, completely eliminate one recurring, variable expense. At the end of this test run, see if you actually missed that expense or not. If so, add it back in; if not, enjoy the money you saved.

CHALLENGE #9:

Understand Your Money Behaviors

I can still remember the first couple of conversations with my husband about our spending habits, my credit card bill, and our collective student loan debt. They were *awful*, emphasis intended. I cried, shut down, got defensive, lashed out, and pretty much did the emotional equivalent of "Eff you, stop talking to me." To me, it felt scary; I wasn't exactly proud of my money habits at the time, and I knew there was a lot I didn't understand or know how to handle. Since I knew my spouse was financially responsible, I worried he would judge me—but really I was just judging myself, and I felt overwhelmed in terms of what changes I needed to make.

Money is emotional, whether you like it or not. Spender or saver with a mind-set of scarcity or abundance, you're probably holding onto some narratives that impact how you make financial decisions, how you handle money as a whole, and what your approach to money might be in the future. This whole challenge will help you dive into some of that, not because I'm a financial coach (I'm most definitely not) but because I've been there; I've asked myself these exact questions, and I can at least provide you with a starting point.

DETERMINE IF YOU'RE A DEFAULT SPENDER OR SAVER

DIFFICULTY LEVEL: **EASY**

How you approach money is deeply rooted in your values, your sense of identity, your upbringing, and your priorities, so understanding your default financial attitude can be helpful in terms of knowing how you're going to react in certain situations or making any necessary changes. Determining if you're a natural spender or saver is an easy way to get started. For example, when you get paid, do you immediately put money aside, or do you go shopping? When you go out to dinner, do you always select whatever you're craving despite the cost, or do you choose something affordable? And if you need to make a larger purchase, do you typically save money to pay for it outright or plunk down your credit card?

For me, it depends on the situation, but I'll shift into spender mode if I'm not careful. That's not necessarily a bad thing, since there are pros and cons to being both. Spenders like to enjoy their money as a way to live life to the fullest, but they might forget to be practical; savers are more patient and future-oriented with purchases, but they may struggle with appreciating their money too. Once you know which way you lean, you can note your blind spots—like if you never treat yourself to anything fun or grimace at investing in a high-quality item, or conversely if you seem to run through money like water and always battle debt of some form. The goal is to find a happy medium, a responsible balance between being frugal and being a spendthrift.

ARTICULATE YOUR PERSONAL MONEY PHILOSOPHY

Experts say most people fall into four "scripts," or philosophies, about money: they avoid it out of anxiety, they believe it's the key to happiness, they try to keep up with others, or they act cautiously. The last script tends to be the healthiest, though it can cause some people to struggle with financial security or avoid ever enjoying what money can buy, and many of these are set early in life as the bedrock of how you spend money as an adult.

I absolutely started in the first camp. I believed I didn't deserve to have a lot of money in life, I would always be subject to debt of some form, and I mostly acted out of anxiety, fear, or avoidance. Like that one time in graduate school when I didn't check my credit card statement for six months in a row, even though I watched the balance climb. I didn't want to see the damage; I wanted to pretend it would go away eventually. These days I view money as a tool that can make life easier, offer fun or enjoyable experiences, and solve certain problems, but it doesn't lead to happiness and it's not the most important thing in life. At the same time, because I've had the experience of money being such a major source of negative emotions, I have to actively give myself permission to spend it now without any guilt.

Knowing your money "script" can help you understand why you spend or save the way you currently do. Furthermore, the financial behaviors we witnessed during childhood may become lessons we later mimic or rebel against—if money was a taboo subject growing up, maybe you avoid talking about it now as an adult, or conversely, maybe you want to be more transparent with your own children and partner. This week think about why money is important to you and how it makes you feel, whether you have enough, don't have enough, or have more than enough. Consider which money script you tend to fall into, what life experiences or circumstances led you to that particular mind-set, and if you want to make a change—or not.

COMPARE YOUR MONEY BEHAVIORS AGAINST YOUR MONEY PHILOSOPHY

As much as I want to have a cautious approach to money, and think that I do for the most part, I also know that's not always true. I can easily shift into impulsive spending, no problem, based on an old scarcity mind-set. Deep down I'm always going to be a little bit afraid of not having enough, which can create some self-destructive or self-sabotaging behaviors, like assuming I'll "never" pay off my debts or being so restrictive that I can't even enjoy lunch out with my husband without feeling guilty. Sometimes how you spend money directly contradicts how you *think* you spend money, and that's why it's important to try to find harmony wherever possible, knowing it's an ongoing dance.

Using some of what you've learned in the other financial challenge exercises, compare all your different money behaviors against what you deem to be your money philosophy. If your money behaviors are a direct contrast to the type of money philosophy you'd like to have—perhaps you frequently overspend, but you really want to be the type of person who can spend money without being plagued with guilt—it's time to make some adjustments.

TRY THIS

Complete the following prompts:

When I spend money, I feel... / When I spend money, I *want* to feel...
When I save money, I feel... / When I save money, I *want* to feel...

Compare the spending and saving statements. Is there a difference between how you currently feel and how you want to feel? What's one thing you can start or stop doing today to make your money behaviors or philosophies better align? Write down the words associated with the way you *want* to feel on a small piece of paper and put it in a location related to spending or saving money, like in your wallet.

CHALLENGE #10:
Live Within Your Means

I'll admit that the phrase "living within your means" automatically makes me think about being limited or feeling deprived, which doesn't sound fun in the least. But the more time I've spent on my own financial habits, the more I've realized that making decisions based on a budget—and being smart about money in general—is a way to live rich. Whether you practice thriftiness and try to spend as little as possible while saving aggressively, or you focus on making money whenever you can to have a bunch of different sources of income, a primary way to live within your means involves fitting your spending into your lifestyle in a way that sets you up for future success.

You don't need to become an utter minimalist either. Just focus on reducing stress around money so you can live more freely. Being in control of your money is powerful—when you know exactly where your money is going and why, you have agency over deciding how to spend it. This challenge provides a few thought exercises that combine sentiments from all the previous money challenges so you can start living a life within your means and *without* financial burden.

IMAGINE YOUR LIFE IF YOU HAD LESS MONEY THAN YOU DO RIGHT NOW

Ten years ago I made about a third of what my take-home pay is now. Though I've definitely matured and learned valuable lessons about how to handle money, I also realize there's not a *huge* difference between how I chose to live then and how I choose to live now. I care about investing in experiences, good food and drink, fewer but better possessions, and the health and security of my family. Back then I appreciated a walk around the block more than going to a movie, and a glass of $3 wine at home on my comfy couch more than going out for a $15 cocktail in a loud restaurant. Those things are still true; however, lifestyle inflation and social media have created a nonstop sense of "keeping up with the Joneses." For example, everywhere I turn online, I see other women with bigger homes, nicer wardrobes, and perfect skin on lavish vacations. And some days those pictures convince me that I need to spend money to change my life—even though I know those highlight reels aren't real.

Reality check: we all know someone who seems better off financially than we are. We're all bound to struggle with FOMO, the fear of missing out on what money can buy, and we're all suspect to comparison and envy—but that's a losing game. Rather than getting accustomed to more, more, more, remember that money doesn't buy happiness, and you can get by on far less than you think. Today imagine your life if you had less money than you do right now. Was there a time when you operated at a very different financial capacity, for better or worse? What was that like? How have things changed since then?

DON'T LIVE PAYCHECK TO PAYCHECK

Huge disclaimer: living paycheck to paycheck is not necessarily an active choice, and plenty of people are in that financial spot for all kinds of legitimate reasons. I'm not here to shame anyone for doing what they need to do to get by based on their circumstances. And if you're living paycheck to paycheck because you're aggressively paying off debt or bulking up your savings, carry on, my friend. But for those of you who get paid on a Friday, spend lavishly for a week, and then nervously wait for the next payday to happen—I'm talking to you. Living paycheck to paycheck means you have enough but just *barely*, which isn't sustainable in the least. It prevents you from saving for your financial goals and investing in your future, because you're always waiting for the next round of income to move the ball forward. It also keeps you on an emotional roller coaster: money comes in (yay!) and then it's gone (no!).

But it doesn't necessarily have to be this way. This week see what you can do to break the cycle. Are you having trouble creating a budget and sticking to it? Sign up for an app or a tool that helps you note spending patterns and track your net worth. Do you need to cut down on spending? Use coupon services or codes, check out secondhand stores or refurbished items, browse clearance racks, and comparison shop to find the best prices. It may take time to create more of a margin in your finances so you're not living paycheck to paycheck, but it's worth it.

CONSIDER WHAT IT LOOKS LIKE, AND FEELS LIKE, TO LIVE WITHIN YOUR MEANS

The phrase "live within your means" will look and feel different for everyone, so this month figure out what it means for *you*. Grab a pen and paper, and use the following questions as a freewriting exercise:

- What does "having enough" mean to you?
- Is there a sum of money that would make you feel content? If so, what is it?
- What is most important to you in terms of spending money? What is least important?

When you live within your means, on your own terms, you feel like you have enough. You set financial goals for the purpose of peace, but not as a way to try to buy happiness. And you're thoughtful about what to spend your money on. So if you're not currently living within your means, use this writing exercise as a way to identify your pain points and figure out if you can make a change—perhaps you used to define "having enough" as having a huge home, but you'd actually like to downsize in order to be able to travel more. Or you'd like to transition from spending *money* on loved ones to spending *time* with them. Whatever the case, start envisioning what living within your means could look like three months from now, and what you can do today to create change.

TRY THIS

For the month ahead, budget from a starting point of zero. Write out every line item with a mind-set of what you "get to" have or do—such as *I get to pay my mortgage to live in this warm home* or *I'm lucky enough to buy toothpaste and paper towels and food at the store whenever I need it*. This flips the perspective of budgeting from something negative, where you have to "sacrifice," to a more positive mentality of gratitude.

Part 5

Career

I've been in the working world for a decade, which means there's still plenty of career lessons left for me to learn. At the same time, I've explored different industries and types of jobs, worked with all sorts of people across the Midwest, earned promotions and raises, and shifted into management. I consistently ask colleagues and friends for advice regarding how they handle their own paths, and I appreciate anyone willing to share insights gleaned from their work, whether it's related to various occupations, side hustles, teams, supervisors, salaries, development opportunities, roles, and responsibilities.

In this section I'll cover the topics that have been most instrumental for my own career journey—like how to own your strengths, take things seriously but not personally, and set boundaries to avoid burnout. We'll also take into account ways you can seek creative challenges, invite feedback, find a mentor, and lead with integrity, just to name a few.

Own Your Talent

Between living in the Midwest and growing up Catholic, humility unsurprisingly became part of my DNA. I had internalized "rules" like these: don't brag, be polite and quiet, don't show off, say thank you, smile and nod, find your place in the background, don't expect too much...along with the assumption that good girls excel while following all these conditions. You know—be smart but not conceited, be funny but not over-the-top, be attractive but don't ask for attention, and so on. Nobody, of course, can truly win this preestablished cultural and societal game—and even those who try end up skewered in some fashion—but it's ridiculously hard to detach yourself too. It took me an awfully long time to realize the power of owning my strengths, skills, and talents. It took me even longer to understand that I could be bold, brave, complex, assertive, and unashamed *without* losing qualities that mattered to me, like grace and respect.

You can own what you're good at and still believe there's more room to learn and grow. You can be confident at work, and still stay open to change. And you don't have to be humble in the traditional sense if it prevents you from harnessing your own fortitude, energy, and power. Here's how.

DETERMINE ONE THING YOU'RE GOOD AT

DIFFICULTY LEVEL:

EASY

Even when I was a little kid, words came easy to me: I talked a lot, made up stories regarding my dolls and stuffed animals, and loved to read and write. In elementary school I legitimately looked forward to English class and library time—to the point where I once got in trouble for sneaking a chapter book under my desk during a science lesson. Writing, for me, felt like doing a brain puzzle where I lost all track of time. I could see and feel the way words needed to fit together to make a point or create sentiment, and I enjoyed the challenge of how to improve my ability to do so based on grammar and style and voice, but also in contrast or comparison to other styles of writing or authors I admired.

Think about one thing you're good at, no questions asked. Be honest with yourself. It doesn't have to be creative in the least, either—maybe you're exceptional at making omelets, or tending to flowers, or finding the best music, or taking long naps, or saying the right thing at exactly the right time to someone in need. No matter what "it" is, it probably comes naturally to you and you gravitate toward doing it, even in hard or discouraging moments. You don't need to make a big, long list, either. Just name one thing that you know, deep down, you bring your A game to, and acknowledge it to yourself.

TRY THIS

Talk to five people who know you really well, and ask them to identify your top strength and biggest weakness. Keep an open mind, and don't get defensive; view it as research! Then add your own responses, and review the list in full. Are there any patterns or duplicates? Do any strengths surprise you, and which weaknesses could you improve or learn from? This should give you at least one strength you can build upon and share with others going forward.

ACCEPT PRAISE FOR YOUR TALENT

Every time I receive a compliment on my writing, I feel a little twinge of discomfort. For a long time, that twinge translated into responses like this: "Oh, thanks...you're so nice! I mean, I'm not *that* good of a writer, I write a lot, but not as much as other people. I'm not, like, a pro or anything. But yeah, I guess I'm decent?" To which the person who gave me the verbal applause stares at me with raised eyebrows, wondering when I'll stop rambling. While I know I'm being awkward about the compliment itself, it feels equally awkward to accept it—because that indicates I agree, God forbid! And think it's true! And oh my stars, to admit you're good at something is just...wrong, right?

Or not. Because on the flip side, when I try to give someone else a compliment, I immediately notice those who accept it with a smile and move on versus those who launch into an odd soliloquy about why they're not deserving of the praise. And that's when, as the person *giving* the compliment, I want to scream, "Dude! Just say thanks. It's okay to be good, hell, *great* at something! Stop with all the justification and backpedaling."

See what it's like to just say thank you—full stop, no song and dance—when someone offers you a compliment or kind word about your talent or gift. Bite your tongue against filling the space just past gratitude with a whole bunch of reasoning, and try to savor (or at least allow) the kudos.

TELL PEOPLE ABOUT YOUR TALENT

You've recognized something you're good at and practiced (hopefully) receiving praise for it in general, and now it's time to test your ability to advocate for yourself. That thing you identified in the easy challenge? Yep, you're going to tell someone, once a week for an entire month, that you're good at it. Here's why: throughout the course of your career, you'll probably run into moments where a project or opportunity arises, and the only way you can be involved is to raise your hand and say, "Hey, I'm actually really good at spreadsheets/speeches/business plans/whatever, and I'd like to be a part of this work." Don't sit there waiting for someone to notice, because even if you do excellent work, people are busy and distracted and thinking about their own needs.

Or think of this exercise as dropping seeds that could later blossom into something fruitful. Once I became a manager, I realized how often I relied on offhand statements people had previously given me regarding what they liked to do or wanted to work on, which absolutely popped up in my brain down the road when I was thinking about how best to delegate a project or give someone a chance. For example, if a person on my team mentioned her strategic mind-set regarding communication plans, you can bet the next time I needed someone to come up with a strategic communication plan, that's who I'd reach out to.

Over the span of the next month, tell four different people what you're good at, your strengths and experiences. This doesn't need to be a formal endeavor; think of it like four opportunities to answer the question "Tell me about yourself." Is there a time when you really pushed yourself outside of your comfort zone and you consequently learned to be resilient in the face of uncertainty? Cool—that might mean you cope well with change. Are you passionate about playing chess? Great—that's really an indicator of your ability to think ahead and build processes. To bypass a feeling of bragging, focus on how the thing you can do well translates to a useful skill or trait that benefits others, and let the people you're telling know that you're practicing how to communicate your strengths.

Take Criticism Seriously, but Not Personally

I first stumbled across this quote, attributed to Hillary Clinton, in a magazine article, and it stopped me dead in my tracks—so much so that I cut it out, scrapbook-style, and pinned it to the bulletin board above my desk. Whatever you think of Clinton the politician, there's no escaping the fact that she's spent the past thirty-plus years navigating a very public career and has probably, in my opinion, learned a thing or two. For me, this quote represents how best to balance your approach to most things at work (not everything, of course, but a lot of situations and people). If I take something seriously, then that means I'm likely listening, considering, and trying to be thoughtful of next steps or contextual information I might need—but if I also take it personally, I might immediately get wrapped up in details that don't matter and find myself unable to see a bigger picture.

Taking criticism seriously, but not personally, allows you to stay calm, focused, and, most of all, resilient in the face of chaos, feedback, or the unexpected. It helps you shift from an emotional reaction— "Oh my God, this will be a disaster" or "I can't believe she said that" —to an action-oriented state of mind—"What do we need to do to minimize the damage here?" or "I want her to know her words were hurtful, but we need to make deadline on this project." And it forces you to either find some merit in the thing itself in order to grow, or let go of what's not useful and move forward.

FIND A PHRASE THAT REMINDS YOU TO DETACH

DIFFICULTY LEVEL: EASY

Let's pretend I'm writing a national speech for an executive leader, something I've done before in my day job. I spend hours and hours on the project completing research, sourcing information, and editing to fit the style of this person as well as provide worthwhile takeaways to the audience at hand. On the day the final draft is due, I hand over the speech, only to be told it's not exactly what the person is looking for, and I need to redo several sections completely. I have two choices. I can take it personally: *Wow, they hate my work... I messed up... I didn't do a good enough job... I really thought this was a smart anecdote... They don't even know how long it takes to put something like this together...* Or I can take it seriously without any of the personal noise in my head: *Hmm, I thought this was on point, but we must have missed a connection somewhere... I can go back to the drawing board, and I'll need more information on that topic to give it another go... I should clarify if the story itself didn't resonate, or if it needs to be replaced entirely...*

In this example it's not that I don't care—I should. It's not that feedback, particularly surprising or negative in nature, is enjoyable to hear—it's usually not. It's not that I don't lament lost hours or worry about bringing my best—I do. And it's not that I approach any task with a laissez-faire attitude of "Welp, whatever happens, happens—not my problem." It's that I've trained myself to pause and remember that it's not about me; it's about the work. That's my go-to phrase, because it reminds me to step back and emphasizes the whole "take things seriously, but not personally" idea. Find a phrase that works for you in the same manner. Think of something you could repeat to yourself in moments like this that could remind you to take work seriously but not personally.

ANALYZE THE CRITICISM FOR TRUTH

Eric Barker, author of *Barking Up the Wrong Tree*, suggests making a list with three columns upon receiving criticism. In the first one, write down exactly what the person said. In the second, write down what you perceive as "wrong" with that feedback. And in the third, write down what might be right. Barker then recommends looking at column three with an observer's mind: ask yourself what you would do if the feedback was indeed true, or how you'd advise a friend to act if he received similar feedback. Chances are there's an element of what's in the third column that might be worth considering if you're able to get past the initial knee-jerk reaction.

Here's another example: a colleague once told me that I emailed too much and needed to make more phone calls for relationship-building. I didn't get along with this person, so I instantly wrote her off as picking on me, and her feedback went in one ear, out the other. But years later I still thought about her words every time I went to either make a phone call or write an email—because I knew, deep down, that she was somewhat right. Calls are more personal, and they're sometimes much more effective than e-communication. The more I grew in my career, the more I could see the wisdom she was trying to offer, even if the delivery came out in an offensive way.

Criticism usually pisses people off because there's a small grain of truth in it somewhere. When someone criticizes you, try Barker's tactic: what *actually* happened (not what you *think* you heard), what seems "wrong" with it, and what might be right. Then look at that third column and give it a little consideration.

TRY THIS

Reflect on an old criticism from your past, one that's stuck with you. Come up with three things you've learned as a result, or ways the experience forced you to grow. You don't have to agree with the criticism; just find the "truth" in it now that a little time has passed.

ACCEPT CRITICISM AS A TOOL FOR GROWTH

DIFFICULTY LEVEL:
HARD

There's an old saying that goes, "To avoid criticism, do nothing, say nothing, and be nothing." Meaning: get over it. Criticism is simply a fact of being a person in the world, and if you spend your entire life trying to stand still as not to ruffle feathers or make sure everybody likes you, congrats—you're being a doormat. What's more, criticism usually serves as an indicator that you're doing *something* worthwhile; you're just also on the journey of incremental progress at the same time. That's why it's entirely possible, and also extremely crucial, to learn how to take criticism seriously, but not personally.

This month, every time you receive feedback or feel judged or find yourself in the position of reacting emotionally, see if you can do one of these things. The key is not to experience criticism and then lock it in a box for another day, but to use it as a tool for growth.

- Did I make a mistake? If so, what do I need to do to resolve it going forward?
- Is this person's opinion valid? If so, how can I take it into account without wanting to go cry in bed for a week?
- Could I have done things differently? If so, what would it look like to try harder or attempt a different path in the future?

Avoid Burnout

At work it's common to talk about how busy you are, as if it's a badge of honor: you're exhausted, you answered emails until midnight, you haven't taken a day off all year. I used to envy those coworkers who darted from meeting to meeting with an ever-packed calendar, who walked into every room texting furiously, laptop and notepad and coffee in hand—they seemed so *important*. Some of that picture I just painted is completely normal and unavoidable, especially the more you advance in your career, and finding balance looks different for everyone. But the older I get, the more I see all that rushing around as the precursor to burnout.

Workplace burnout isn't simply a random bad day, though; it's an extended period of stress with very real physical, mental, and emotional consequences. Noticing the symptoms can help you avoid burnout entirely as well as figure out the best way to set boundaries as a whole. If you're feeling out of control and overly negative and lacking motivation at work, here are three things you can do.

IDENTIFY YOUR WARNING SIGNS

There are plenty of days where I don't really feel like working, I have trouble getting started on a project, or I experience stress or frustration in my career—and all of those are a natural side effect of any job, in my opinion. However, this is where burnout can easily creep in if I'm not careful. I'm tired one week, but then I start to feel completely spent or disinterested every single day. One blip of stress shifts into a constant attitude of "I don't matter" or "Nobody even cares if this gets done"; momentary distraction starts to feel chronic, where I can't really concentrate or pay attention. I start thinking about work all the time, which gets in the way of my ability to be present with friends or family members, or practice self-care outside of work hours. You get the idea.

Over time I've learned to take action as soon as these warning signs appear: I shut down my computer whenever possible, head out for a walk or a yoga class, spend time doing something completely unrelated to work, and basically give myself permission to back off in order to hit the reset button. I know that in a state of burnout, there's no way to perform the way I want to in my career, and even if it feels like I should push through or carry on, the best thing I can do for myself is to stop and rest.

Knowing what burnout looks like and feels like for you specifically is key to managing it, so pay close attention to those little indicators—inability to sleep, moodiness, problems disconnecting—that can lead to something more serious.

ESTABLISH SOME BOUNDARIES

As soon as I shifted into a managerial role, I began to feel burned out. I stressed about the avalanche of emails in my inbox. Every time someone on my team stopped by for "just a minute," I had to take a deep breath. No room for thinking or doing seemed to exist on my calendar, only meetings and conference calls. And when I got home at the end of the day, I either kept worrying about work or wanted to get into bed and go to sleep right away.

Not good. I had to set some new boundaries. I scheduled blocks of time every day to do my own tasks, strategic or tactical, and said no to certain meetings or calls that weren't necessarily a priority. I tried to clear almost every Friday, too, to give myself a specific day to either play catch-up, be creative, or think critically about our team responsibilities and deliverables. Since I had an actual office, I shut my door when I was working on key projects so I wouldn't be distracted or interrupted. I asked my direct reports to give me twenty-four to forty-eight hours to respond to requests unless they were urgent, but I committed to checking in with them every day in person at least once. I also tried to stop working through my lunch break at least a few times a week; instead I went to a yoga class or stepped outside for a walk or actually ate my food without multitasking. And in the course of a couple of weeks, I felt immensely better and more capable of handling anything that came my way.

To me, boundaries are the little sister of balance: approachable, realistic, friendly. Balance always sounds so elusive and perfect, but it's really hard to obtain and even more difficult to maintain over time. Boundaries, however, are doable strategies to help you manage both work and home so you can function at your best. And when you're experiencing burnout, you've likely failed to set or preserve the boundaries that allow you to protect your time and energy. This week pick one or two things that support your ability to work hard *and* smart.

BE PROACTIVE

Soon after I received a promotion at work, I felt bogged down by emails, but I couldn't seem to get ahead. I consequently spent the better part of a week responding to work emails at 10 p.m. until one of my colleagues replied back by saying, "Thanks for this. Now get off your laptop and hang out with your family. Work will be here tomorrow." That exchange stuck with me. Now, I briefly check email at night, just in case anything major comes up, but I don't tackle anything that can wait until the next day. When I'm at the office, I set dedicated times throughout the day to check email so it doesn't pile up. That allows me to stay connected without falling behind but also maintain a healthier work-life balance.

It's so incredibly easy to stay in productive beast mode, especially in certain industries—but if you don't address burnout, it will seriously impact your health. I'm talking fatigue, insomnia, relationship issues, depression or anxiety, and even illnesses like heart disease, high cholesterol, and obesity in the long run. The good news? You can treat and address burnout symptoms on your own or with the help of a doctor or mental healthcare provider. I've also found it helpful to share feelings of burnout with the people around you: tell your coworkers that you're struggling, ask your supervisor if there are options to better manage any job stressors, and encourage your friends and family members to support behaviors that promote healthy boundaries. Reorganize your calendar, take more breaks or time off, review your job description to see if anything needs to change, and get plenty of sleep, healthy eats, and exercise.

TRY THIS

Look at your schedule for the next seven days, and make sure there's at least fifteen minutes to an hour of built-in downtime every day. Literally pencil it in, and view it as a nonnegotiable part of your week. Share your plan with a friend or coworker, and ask that person to help hold you accountable. At the end of the week, see if your burnout symptoms have subsided at all.

CHALLENGE #4:
Seek Creative Challenges

When I was a kid, if my sisters and I told our mom that we were bored, she would wave her hands and say, "If you're bored, you're boring." Meaning: go find something to do. After some moaning and groaning, our creative juices would slowly kick in: we'd build a fort using blankets and the kitchen table, outline an entire city for our Barbies and Beanie Babies across couches and end tables, and swing outside while perusing the grass for tiny flowers. My mother's reaction taught me to view boredom as a temporary state of mind, one I had complete control over, and the same is true for adults as well as children.

It's easy to think of creativity as something reserved for a special few: the artists, the dreamers, the entrepreneurs. Or maybe you think of creative output only as something with significant impact: coming up with the Next Big Thing or wild innovation in your industry. But it's really related to moving outside your comfort zone. New challenges position you to grow, which is imperative for you personally, and from a career perspective, your growth and development increase your value—which is good for job security and for your long-term potential as a whole. This challenge is all about how you can continually find ways to level up in your career in terms of proactively pushing yourself creatively.

PURSUE ONE "WHAT IF" THOUGHT

DIFFICULTY LEVEL:

EASY

One thing I admire about my husband is his eagerness to explore new skills. He's the type of person who will wake up at 3 a.m. thinking of ways to solve a coding problem. He honors his "what if" thoughts and inspires me to do the same, and he's also taught me that this type of thinking can show up in many ways.

For example, I once worked with a team of marketing folks, and we kept running into the problem of identifying publication channels. I remember thinking, *I wish we had a database of all these newsletters that everyone could access.* I brought it up to some leaders and asked what they thought, and they agreed—yeah, sounds great. This type of task wasn't in my job description, nor did anyone request that I personally make it happen. But I could see the value, so I did it. Then when someone had a question, I pointed to the database. Is that example particularly *creative*? Nah. Still, any time you bring something into existence that didn't exist before, you're strengthening your creative skills because you're looking for gaps, asking questions, clarifying pain points, and taking initiative.

Your challenge today? See if you can go with your "What if?" impulse the tiniest bit, even if the concept at hand seems beyond challenging, out of scope for your talent or role, or too pie-in-the-sky. Stay curious, and consider if there's any way you could work toward that thought in some capacity, or at least open the door to conversation about such work with the right people.

TRY THIS

Set a timer for two minutes. Write down the phrase "I wish I knew how to..." and then finish that sentence with however many examples come to mind. Keep writing until the timer goes off. Pick one thing on the list you could explore creatively this week. For example, if you wrote, "I wish I knew how to speak French," then borrow a beginner's book from the library or watch a few introductory videos online. Anything new or different will feel like a creative challenge!

ROTATE A RESPONSIBILITY WITH SOMEONE

My current colleagues and I like to joke about how we're experts at maternity leave coverage, because nearly every woman on our small team has had at least one baby. While some of that process is completely unavoidable—the work has to get done, so it's usually all hands on deck in terms of who can cover what—it's also taught me the value of cross-functionality. In other words, job rotation can help you learn and develop new or different skills, earn a better sense of how hard or detailed job responsibilities might be, gain a better appreciation for the expertise of others, and cultivate a broader viewpoint on how your team, department, or organization functions. Here's why: when you first take a role, you spend the first year or so trying to achieve specialization, or get really good at what you were hired to do. This makes total sense, but after you gain confidence in those abilities, you might start to look for other responsibilities to support the breadth and depth of your current skills. And before you leap toward a potential promotion or go on the job hunt yet again for a supposed "new challenge," it's worth looking *around* at what your teammates are doing.

Step out of your specific role this week, and ask if there's a task you could trade or rotate with a colleague, friend, or partner. Ideally it's related enough to your daily work or baseline skill set so that you don't need a ton of training to give it a go—for example, you're in editorial and feeling a little stagnant regarding your usual "beat" of stories, so you and a coworker swap the types of assignments you normally take this week to liven things up. This type of switch gives you ample opportunity to be creative and experiment with work you don't normally handle.

SET A CREATIVE GOAL

My creative goals at work often revolve around amplifying the skills I'm already good at—like improving my writing in a certain way or trying a new editorial calendar software program. That is wonderful, but sometimes I have to remind myself (for the millionth time) that the most important growth comes when I get out of my established "box." Easier said than done, right? One year, however, I realized every time a report arrived from our social and digital teams, my eyes sort of glazed over at all the numbers; I *mostly* understood it but also...didn't. Not fully. It wasn't imperative that I know the ins and outs of each report for my daily work; however, I also knew that simply nodding my head in agreement wouldn't do me any favors in the long run.

In response, along with a few specialists on our team, I decided to get certified in Google Analytics; we got together on a weekly basis for an hour to run through the lessons together. It was hard and made me feel like a fish out of water. But by the end of the course, we were all better able to understand ways to collect and process data, how different metrics provided different layers of context or value, the benefits of various analysis tools, targeting strategies, measuring goals, and campaign tracking. Did that knowledge change my day-to-day? Not really. Was I equipped to ask better questions of our digital and social teams, and make more thoughtful, creative recommendations regarding content strategy? You bet.

This month set a creative goal around something you've always wanted to learn how to do at work, or at least something that you *know* will be beneficial.

CHALLENGE #5:

Don't Be the Brilliant Jerk

The worst experience of my career thus far involved a coworker who fit the classic "brilliant jerk" stereotype: exceptionally talented, capable of delivering significant results to the bottom line, and a grade A bully. This person consistently caused drama on our team, criticized my every move with relish, and took a my-way-or-the-highway approach to nearly every single project. Unfortunately, the behavior was excused—whenever I tried to talk to my supervisor about the problem, I received a grimace and a reason why I needed to cut this colleague some slack due to a bad day or stress or God knows what. Eventually the environment became so toxic that I left. To this day, when I think of how *not* to act at work, I think of her.

And I consequently have zero tolerance for such bullshit. I don't care how smart or talented you are—treating people, regardless of role or title, with respect, compassion, and professionalism is essential. What's more, a 2015 Harvard Business School study indicated that avoiding hiring these types of toxic workers is worth about $12,500 in turnover costs, which doesn't even include other potential costs ranging from litigation fees to low employee morale. There's a very real impact to an organization, a team, and your career as an individual when brilliant jerks are around.

I know, I know—you're probably thinking, *Okay, well that's not me.* That may be true. But it's actually pretty easy to slide into brilliant jerk territory if you're not careful. You use the strategies in this challenge to be mindful of your attitude at work, understand why toxic team members are so harmful to your career, and learn how to manage anyone who fits this description.

DECIDE WHAT TYPE OF ATTITUDE YOU WANT TO BE KNOWN FOR

There's a quote I've always loved, attributed to artist Francesca Reigler, that goes like this: "Happiness is an attitude. We either make ourselves miserable, or happy and strong. The amount of work is the same." Basically choose your attitude: not every day is going to be easy or even enjoyable, but you have the power to decide how you want to approach whatever comes your way, the good and the bad.

For example, the other day I received a phone call from a coworker who was upset about a number of issues related to the work of my team. I spent most of the conversation listening to her tell me how she had been wronged, what she thought should've happened, and what she believed I needed to do next—all in a passive-aggressive tone of "I'm right, you're wrong." When we finally got off the phone, a wave of irritation rushed over me, and I responded by grumbling about her to my coworkers and dismissing her claims. I'll be honest; it felt good...until it felt kind of wrong. I couldn't control her, but I could definitely manage my own attitude in a productive way. I didn't need to be perfect—everyone has to be able to let off steam in difficult situations—but I did need to be more interested in finding solutions and behaving in a way I felt proud of, rather than expanding the negativity to other people.

Today watch how your attitude ebbs and flows. It's not about being phony or overly positive; think through how you want to show up in your career. I want to be known as someone who generally reacts to any situation with grace. What about you?

TRY THIS

Think of three people whose attitude you admire and why. On a note card, write down a word that describe each person's demeanor, and put the card someplace visible in your workspace. Every time you see it, use those words as motivation to be your best self.

REALIZE THE REPERCUSSIONS OF A BAD ATTITUDE

I've known plenty of people who've credited a lousy attitude to being blunt, telling it like it is, problems at home, stress, being fact-oriented, or anything. But sometimes people *like* being Negative Nancy, for reasons I'll never fully understand, and claim they "don't care what anyone else thinks," which makes me laugh because, uh, you *should* care. Caring is cool and niceness pays dividends. No matter your talent, if you act like a jerk, then people eventually view you as harder to work with, so they avoid engaging your skills unless absolutely necessary or they dread collaborating with you—both of which impact culture, productivity, efficiency, and results. When you act like a jerk, you hurt the team and the company, and you create a tone that can lessen the motivation of others. Ultimately you either care about *not* doing those things, or you don't.

Obviously we're all susceptible to losing our tempers and saying the wrong thing. I remember snapping at a coworker who asked for help with an assignment, telling them to Google the question at hand. Later I felt like a jerk—because I was being a jerk! I could've delivered that perspective in a much more constructive way, and since I didn't, the result had a ripple effect: the coworker stopped reaching out to me, the question didn't get answered, and I created unnecessary bad vibes in the office. I knew better and apologized accordingly.

This week, whether it's your attitude that flares up or someone else's, notice the side effects: How does it impact you directly? Your team or coworkers? The work itself? And how would a different approach have led to a more constructive end result?

WHEN FACED WITH A BRILLIANT JERK, SPEAK UP

Okay, so *you're* not the brilliant jerk; you've got your attitude in check and you're bringing your best self to the table each day. Awesome. What happens, though, if you happen to work with someone who does qualify as a brilliant jerk?

Call. Them. Out. And then talk to a supervisor or boss or leader you trust.

Yes, it'll be hard. Yes, you'll probably feel uncomfortable. Yes, you might be like, "Well, it was one time..." or "I don't want to get involved" or "This isn't really my place." And I encourage you to speak up anyway, not because it will necessarily get rid of the brilliant jerk or solve any related problems, but because it's important for the long-term health of your career. When you craft the ability to identify a bad attitude, the next step is holding yourself and those around you accountable to showing up differently. That means being brave enough to say, "The way you're speaking to me right now is unacceptable." And "I don't appreciate your tone; it's rude and doesn't help us solve the problem at hand or move this work forward." And "Hey, Boss Lady/Man? I want you to know that So-and-So is repeatedly negative in a certain situation, and it's preventing our team from doing our best work." By speaking up and showing up, you're representing your values through boundaries. One of my biggest regrets from that experience I shared at the start of this challenge is the fact that I stayed silent the vast majority of the time; I was too scared to confront the jerk in the office, and it consequently took a toll on my self-confidence and self-worth. Don't do the same. Speak up.

CHALLENGE #6:
Ask for More

In my first three jobs out of college, I did everything in my power to be a fantastic employee. I showed up on time. I took on extra responsibilities whenever the opportunity arose. I kept my head down and delivered projects on time. I did my best to be polite, reliable, hardworking, and honest. And then I waited, based on the assumption that if I did all of the "right" things you're supposed to do at a job, then someone would notice my talent, give me more money, hand over a promotion, or all of the above. Which isn't exactly how it works. (Though it sounds lovely!) Although I have had the benefit of an excellent boss or two who championed a raise or title change on my behalf, for the most part you have to ask for more instead of waiting around for someone to do it for you. Here are three tips I've learned over the years that have successfully taught me how to take advantage of opportunities, clarify what I want at work, and advocate for my worth.

BE SPECIFIC AND DIRECT WHEN YOU ASK FOR AN OPPORTUNITY

Delete the phrase "Let me know if I can help" from your vocabulary. Technically there's nothing wrong with this phrase: it indicates a willingness to offer support. It also isn't helpful in the least. When you tell someone to let you know if you can help, you put all of the work on them; they now have to identify where they need an extra hand, explain what you can do along with the how and why, and then communicate all of that back to you.

Look at the following examples:

- **Not helpful:** "Let me know if I can help with any of the applications."
- **Better:** "There are three application deadlines coming up. Do you want me to look at these?"
- **Best:** "I noticed we have several application deadlines in the next month, and your plate is pretty full. I'm actually very interested in becoming more knowledgeable in this space, and due to my experience on X project, I'd love to prep these and bring them back to you for review this week so we can stay on target. Does that work for you?"

Let's discuss why number three is ideal. The first one is still a version of "let me know," so nix that. With the second you're being slightly more specific but still asking for permission to do work in a way that'll put the onus on your boss to figure out how to respond and what to do. In the third you're indicating that you pay attention to detail and what work needs to be done, you've thought about *why* you want to work on this specific project, you offer an action-oriented solution that keeps your boss involved, and you reinforce the fact that this approach is efficient, productive, or good for the company.

Being specific and direct when you ask for an opportunity positions you for a "yes."

IDENTIFY WHAT YOU WANT MORE OF

Most people find it challenging to clarify exactly what they want at work, at least when it comes to money, a title change or promotion, or responsibilities. At various points in my career thus far, I struggled to determine which one I wanted: *Yes, more money is always nice, but can I really ask for that amount right now? I'd love to manage people, but am I qualified to do that yet? I'm interested in learning about the strategic work of the company, but isn't that just for people with certain titles?* Sometimes it felt like all three, and sometimes one seemed glaringly necessary.

This week think about what you want more of at work and why. Are you feeling stagnant in terms of the type of work you're doing? Are your contributions undervalued, and you want your pay to better align with the quality of your work? Do you need a flexible schedule or different hours? What projects are a great use of your skill set, and what are examples of work that could be shifted to someone else's portfolio?

TRY THIS

Do a mini career-mapping exercise. Think about your career now and where you'd like it to go in the next twelve months. Write down two things: what you need more of and what you need less of. From there, parcel out one tangible, proactive thing you could do each quarter (every three months) to make those adjustments.

ADVOCATE FOR YOUR WORTH

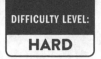

Asking for more can translate to a bunch of different things, but for most of the people I talk to, asking for more frequently involves money as a form of advocating for your worth: negotiating salaries, working toward bonuses, asking for a raise, and confirming the right combination of favorable benefits. And these conversations are some of the hardest to navigate.

It's only recently in my career that I've pushed myself to not only discuss pay with friends, coworkers, clients, and employers but also become more comfortable being my own spokesperson for what I think I deserve. For example, I spent the first year of freelance writing thrilled with whatever anyone would pay me, if they paid me anything at all. As I gained more experience, I started to realize that I could ask for more money—or at least identify the income I needed to receive in order to match the value of the time spent on these assignments.

Would that approach have worked if I didn't have the skill and years of experience to back it up? Of course not—it's important to be mindful and realistic regarding what you think you deserve; pick your battles and meet people halfway. But advocating for your worth at work, whether that involves pay, schedule, or responsibilities, is how you can slowly get comfortable with asking for more in general.

CHALLENGE #7:
Invite Feedback

According to PricewaterhouseCoopers (PwC), almost 60 percent of employees said they'd like feedback from their bosses on a daily or weekly basis. Why, then, do so many people dread getting feedback, or get defensive and upset in the face of it? Well, it's personal—most people genuinely want to do a great job at work, and receiving constructive criticism can feel intensely personal, like a label of "sorry, not good enough." However, feedback is necessary if you want to learn, change, and grow, and without it you're more susceptible to professional blind spots.

That's why asking for feedback, rather than waiting until a supervisor or colleague offers it up, is a proactive way to do a pulse check. Doing so shows confidence and an interest in improving yourself in order to take advantage of your full potential. It also indicates you're committed to your team or organization, and to making your work the best it can be.

ADMIT YOUR DEFAULT REACTION TO FEEDBACK

When I first started teaching yoga classes at a studio, it was common practice for more experienced instructors to attend and then provide feedback afterward. After class one day, one of my mentors who had attended asked if we could chat for a minute. My stomach sank a little bit, but I nodded. He then asked that I hold my responses until he finished, and really listen to what he had to say instead of immediately jumping in with my reaction or opinion. I said yes, thinking that sounded like no big deal. But the second he started talking, I wanted, more than anything, to interrupt, defend, and explain. Although I thought I would have the wherewithal to hold steady, it turns out my default reaction was to rationalize—big-time. My ego desperately wanted to describe why I made every single decision of that class, and I had to take deep breaths to wait out his words.

That experience illustrated the fact that I wasn't actually very good at receiving feedback. Like, at all. I've spent years working on this quality, and even now I still have to hold my tongue and mentally tell myself to pause and listen before allowing my brain to race ahead with assumptions and reactions. I also usually need to take some space from a feedback conversation in order to let what someone else is trying to tell me fully settle in.

Lots of people like to think they're good at reacting to feedback, but let's be real: we're not. We get defensive, we feel pissed off, we turn into stone, we lash out, we rationalize, and so on. Very few of us welcome feedback with open arms and a big smile, at least not at first. Today think back on a time you received feedback, and be really honest with yourself about how you truly responded, even if it wasn't the best.

ASK YOUR BOSS OR A COLLEAGUE FOR FEEDBACK

You probably wait until your annual performance review to see if your boss has feedback to give. If it's positive, you celebrate the win; if it's negative, you decide you're a crap human being. Ranging between these two extremes is exhausting and, honestly, not super helpful. Instead, here are two middle ground options that can be incredibly useful.

First, listen. Let the other person talk, and take their words with a grain of salt. You can sift out what's useful and what's not later on; you also have permission to decide if you agree or disagree. Feedback is subjective, and it's *one* person's perspective or opinion. The second option, per bestselling author Ramit Sethi, is all about testing theories and assumptions. To change a behavior, says Sethi, you have to operationalize it, and the best way to do that is through systematic testing to see what's true and what's not. Let's say your boss tells you to be more assertive at work. Your initial reaction might be defensive, or your mind may bounce through a bunch of excuses. Using Sethi's philosophy of testing, you have some choices. You can ignore the feedback, or you can practice being assertive for a short period of time, just to see how it feels. Basically, whatever feedback you get, you try it on for size before determining the value or correctness of the feedback.

This week ask for pointed feedback from your boss or colleague on a specific project or assignment. Listen to what the person has to say without responding, and then try testing it.

TRY THIS

Set up fifteen minutes with a trusted coworker or your supervisor to discuss feedback on one particular issue or area. Give the person enough information beforehand so she has a little time to prepare. During the session, take notes and do more listening than speaking. Send a follow-up email to thank the person afterward, and then check in over the next few months to let the person know how you're applying the feedback in a constructive way.

OFFER RESPECTFUL AND CONSTRUCTIVE FEEDBACK

In her book *Radical Candor*, Kim Scott coins a term by the same title and defines it as the ability to care personally and challenge directly. Based on her experiences leading sales and operations at Google, teaching leadership seminars at Apple, and coaching the CEOs of tech companies, Scott talks extensively about how giving and receiving feedback is one of the hardest things anyone can do, but one of the most valuable. We've spent a little bit of time in the easy and medium challenges discussing how to better receive feedback, and now it's worth considering how (and how often) you give feedback to others as well. You might assume giving feedback isn't your job or your place, especially if you aren't a manager or hold a certain title. That's not true; learning how to offer respectful, constructive feedback is important for any role, any job, any company, and really any life situation.

Practice giving feedback to someone. Start by asking if you can share feedback so the other person feels mentally prepared to accept what you're about to say. Emphasize that you want to learn from the discussion and that your goal isn't to criticize the person you're talking to, but to find a solution or better understand how to move forward. And be open to whatever happens in response, which you certainly can't control. The more you give feedback and witness different types of reactions to feedback, the more you'll be encouraged to think about your own reactions too—both of which assist your professional growth, maturity, and ability to show up as a top performer.

CHALLENGE #8:
Take No Shortcuts

I frequently receive emails with a request to "grab coffee" or "pick my brain" about writing or becoming a writer. Half of me doesn't mind—I certainly understand the interest in connecting with someone who is doing work you'd like to do, and I benefited from the advice and guidance of other writers early on as well. The other half of the time, I feel exasperated, simply because it's clear the requester didn't put much thought into the ask; I have no clue how I can actually help, and it seems like the person really just wants me to describe a shortcut to success...when there isn't one. I mean, I love a good caffeinated meet-up for the right reasons, but there are also only so many hours in the day, and with a family, a full-time job, and deadlines to meet, I want to maximize my time and energy too. Similarly, in an office environment, I struggle every time I'm asked a question where it's evident the answer could've been found from, um, a quick Internet search or just a little critical thinking.

It's not that I'm uninterested in being supportive or helpful. It's just that most people don't take a few minutes to put forth a little effort, or they don't necessarily think through what they actually need from the person they're asking. In this challenge we'll talk about why this is problematic, and I'll share a couple of mental strategies you can use to think through any ask.

USE THE "DID YOU LOOK?" CHECKPOINT

Growing up, if my sisters and I couldn't find something—school paper-work, a favorite pair of shoes, car keys—we'd often ask our parents. My mom usually joined us in the hunt, noting where she last saw the missing item, but my dad invariably said one thing: "Did ya look?" This was incredibly annoying as a teenager, of course, and resulted in eye rolls and puffy sighs of indignation. In my head, *of course* I had looked everywhere, duh, that's why I was *asking*. Then, three out of four times, the item in question ended up being exactly where it belonged... I just hadn't looked very hard. Memories like that make me laugh now, since I was being such a typical young adult. Still, my dad's question lingers in my ears every time I can't figure out a problem, find an answer, or resolve an issue: "Did ya look?" It reminds me to try looking first, because the thing I'm looking for is probably more obvious than I think.

Today use that question as a checkpoint for every roadblock or question that arises. Have you gone through old files and saved emails? Is there an answer in an online forum? Has anyone on your team dealt with this before? What might the solution entail, and what pieces of that solution can you handle on your own? Are there bits of information you already have that you can use to make an educated guess? If you need to ask for help, what exactly do you need help with? Overall, did you look?

TRY THIS

For the next week, every time you're about to ask someone a question, ask yourself this question first: *Have I done everything in my power to figure this out on my own?* If the answer is no, back up, wait an hour or a day (depending on the situation), and do your due diligence. If you still need help, reach out, but start by explaining what you've done to try to find a solution.

DO YOUR HOMEWORK

After I accepted my very first freelance gig, I realized I needed some support from fellow writers. But I didn't know any in my city until I met Cassie, a writer and photographer at the same website I had just begun to write for. I emailed her and basically said, "Hi, can I buy you coffee and talk writing?"

When we got together, we immediately hit it off. I asked her all sorts of questions about her pitch process, experience with certain publishing teams, and social media strategy. Here's what I didn't say: "Will you share your contact list with me?" or "What story ideas do you have that I could maybe use?" Because, duh. Her talent and her successful bylines were a by-product of hard work. And while I wanted her professional input, I also knew that I had to do my own homework too.

Before you ask for help this week, consider if you've done your homework first. If not, dive into that first. Research articles on the topic at hand, borrow a book from the library, look up other experts to see what they've done, find examples of what you're trying to do, and clarify exactly what questions you have where you do need some additional direction. Do all of that before making an ask for someone else's time.

OUTLINE YOUR REQUEST BEFORE MAKING IT

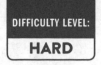

DIFFICULTY LEVEL:

HARD

I recently scheduled a feedback session with a leader who has been both a mentor and a friend. The week before the meeting, I set aside a few minutes to strategically think through what I needed from her and what I hoped to walk away with. I wrote down three areas for which I wanted her specific feedback, either positive or negative, and then I listed one management question I had where I wanted her personal advice. Then, because I expected she'd probably ask *me* for feedback in return, I identified two things she's done really well since we've worked together, and two areas where our relationship could be improved. Did I plan to use all of that in the meeting, verbatim? No. But it helped me organize my thoughts and functioned as a conversation outline I could use to make the most of our time—and *her* time as a busy vice president and mom of three. I wanted to be prepared.

The intent around avoiding shortcuts isn't to warn you against ever asking for help; in fact, it's the opposite. Instead focus on all the legwork you can do up front before reaching out, because that's how you'll be most successful and truly receive the support, advice, and guidance you need. This month take a minute every time you need to ask for help to think about what you're really trying to do and if you've done your due diligence. Organizing those thoughts, and putting forth some initial effort, will go a long way.

Rethink Your Approach to Mentorship

Young professionals are told over and over again to acquire a mentor for professional success, but in my experience it's a lot harder than it sounds—at least based on the classic model. I grew up assuming a mentor was your boss's boss, or at least someone much older and wiser than you within your same industry or company, and entirely based on a formalized relationship. I pictured going to coffee with this person, receiving advice and instruction, and then putting that feedback into practice. I never once thought about the fact that this type of one-to-one coaching sucks up a huge amount of time and energy, so anyone likely to be a great mentor is likely hesitant to invest for free, or able to support only a couple of people at a time. I also didn't consider the difference between a mentor and a sponsor: the former functions as a source of guidance and advice, but maybe not as an advocate or someone directly in your corner, while the latter can be anyone who recognizes your work ethic in way that improves your connections or visibility.

This challenge introduces a modern approach to mentorship: how you can line yourself up with people already on your side, be flexible in figuring out who and what might best serve your career goals, and start to establish the seedlings of such relationships.

CONSIDER THE PEOPLE ALREADY ON YOUR SIDE

My direct supervisor in my day job over the past five years has shepherded my growth, pushed me to perform, encouraged my development as a manager, and consistently urged me to speak up and step up. My parents never fail to remind me to try harder and dream bigger, and my husband quietly and consistently supports every new initiative I want to explore. I look to one friend for writing advice when I need editorial insights on a particular story. And I have peers who I check in with regarding career skills and compensation trajectories as a whole. The point is that I don't have just one person to mentor me, and the older I get, the more I realize the benefits of casting a wide net.

Likewise, career coach Kathy Caprino recommends viewing the people you're already working with as potential mentors, rather than trying to "find" one. She suggests keeping three things in mind:

1. Who already knows how you communicate and contribute?
2. Who trusts you?
3. Who is likely to believe you'll put their feedback to good use?

You're looking to build upon an existing relationship, because that'll give the potential mentor in question more of a reason to invest her time and energy in helping you succeed. Mentors don't have to be coworkers or leaders at work, either; they can be friends, family, or people you know through sidebar activities or community organizations or volunteer week. You can learn and grow from really anyone, so instead of trying to build a mentor relationship from scratch, start with who you know.

TRY THIS

Ask a few people in your network if they have a mentor, how that relationship came about, and what they've learned from the experience. Those takeaways might be useful later on as you try to establish a connection with a potential mentor.

DETERMINE WHAT YOU'RE LOOKING FOR IN A MENTOR

Having a mentor sounds good, like a worthwhile box to check on your career journey, but eventually you'll need to think hard about *why* you want someone to mentor you in any capacity, and what exactly you're looking to gain from that type of relationship, whether short-term or long-term. Here's a quick-hit list of questions to contemplate:

- Do you want someone to help you work on a new project?
- Do you need someone to act as a sounding board or give straight-forward advice when you're struggling to make a decision or handle a specific situation?
- Are you interested in relationships built on a phone call here or there? Short emails back and forth? Lunch or coffee a few times a year?
- Is your intent to find someone whose career path you can mirror?
- Are there access points or connections you're missing, and are you hoping to benefit from someone else's?

Use the list you created in the easy challenge and identify who already fills what need. From there, see if there are any major gaps where you could indeed use another mentor or sponsor. Or perhaps you don't need a relationship at all, and you can get the inspiration, advice, and connections you're seeking through a networking group, a blogging community, or resources like podcasts, books, and conferences. The goal of any type of mentorship is to help you progress, not act as your therapist or tell you what to do. Finally, the best types of mentor relationships happen naturally; they're not forced or overly crafted, and they exist best when both people feel invested and like they're giving as much as they're getting.

INVEST IN POTENTIAL MENTORS

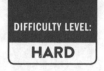

Mentor relationships, like friendships, ebb and flow. Some might last a lifetime or a lifelong career path, while others meet your needs for a short period of time and then fade out. That's why it's a good idea to continually be on the lookout for new or different people you'd love to learn from. Be open to whoever you spark with, not in a romantic sense but in a "Wow, I admire what they're doing, and I want to be a part of it, see how I can help, support their work, or ask for their insights." Again, because it's a two-way street, you should also think about how your own connections, skills, and experiences might prove valuable or indispensable to them too.

I also use the word *invest* deliberately here. It likely won't work to go up to someone you hope to have as a mentor and say, "Can you be my mentor?" It'll feel overly formal, and a little icky or transactional. Instead seek to build connection through repeated interactions, find common ground, and be transparent about how you're looking to grow. Think of these potential relationships as just that: relationships you'd like to invest in, not something you check off your to-do list. Reaching out to more than one person is a way to sidestep putting all your eggs in one basket too—someone may want to help you but truly doesn't have the capacity right then, or another person might forget to respond to your email request. Put out a lot of feelers, over and over again, and be patient. Be willing to invest your own time and energy first before you ask someone to act accordingly.

No matter where your career path leads you, the number one thing to hold onto is a sense of integrity. To me, this involves waking up each morning feeling like I truly did my best, made decisions based on honesty and principle, and behaved with positive intent toward the people in my life. It means I'm proud of my effort, regardless of outcome or mistakes or success. Integrity is something that I control—nobody can take it away from me unless I let them—and it's what I rely on as an ethical compass in times of struggle, confusion, or difficulty.

Other people seem to feel the same way. A 2016 survey by Robert Half Management Resources cited integrity as the single most important leadership attribute, followed closely by fairness and collaboration. It makes sense: if you believe a person has integrity, you're more likely to trust him, view him as competent and kind, and practice commitment. I also find it interesting that integrity generally has very little to do with job titles or positions held. Figuring out how best to align your decisions with your own personal values, thinking through the consequences of any decision, and making choices based on the kind of future you want are some of the most important things you'll ever do—whether it's related to your career, your relationships, your health, your education, or your faith. In this challenge we'll talk about the importance of appreciating others, holding yourself accountable, and using integrity as a tool to build character.

APPRECIATE, THANK, AND CELEBRATE OTHERS

After a few extremely successful months with freelance writing, a friend sent me a card in the mail that simply said, "I'm so proud of you for following your passion on your own terms." Our Realtor, of all people, shared an article I had written to her social media accounts and gave me high praise for including one of her best tips. I received flowers from my boss, our department vice president, and the CEO of the company I work for, all to applaud a major writing gig I landed—which, of course, has nothing to do with my day-to-day responsibilities related to each of them. And one of my best friends told me how much she loved seeing me feel "happy, accomplished, and validated in the art of my choice." Being recognized and supported by these people wasn't expected or even necessary, but it reminded me of the power of celebrating wins, and how much recognizing other people matters. These moments made me feel so special and seen and valued—and they reminded me to do exactly the same for others whenever possible.

Career success is never just about you anyway. It's the coworkers who help you reach a certain target, give thoughtful input on a dilemma, or stay late to pull pieces of a project together. It's the front desk assistant who always makes sure the doors are open and unlocked at the right times, or the intern who runs the numbers and ducks out to pick up lunch orders. It's your spouse or partner or family member who watches your kids so you can fit in an extra hour of work, or sleep in due to being exhausted from the previous week. The more you appreciate, thank, and celebrate the people who make your success possible, the more you demonstrate integrity, because you recognize it takes a village to get, well, anywhere in life. So today take a moment to do just that: appreciate someone, thank someone, and celebrate someone.

HOLD YOURSELF
ACCOUNTABLE

The leaders I know who practice integrity are usually the first to admit they're wrong, and that's one of the qualities I admire most and strive to emulate. Part of leading and living with integrity includes mistakes: you mess up, you experience a lapse in judgment, you totally drop the ball. And that's okay, so long as those moments are followed by an apology, taking ownership or admitting fault, and finding solutions—all of which support your credibility. Way too often in today's landscape, we see people in positions of leadership and power whose integrity is exactly zilch; they say and do whatever it takes to get ahead, look good, and protect their own interests. Most of the time, these individuals are the last in line with respect to accountability. The blame is always placed elsewhere and a finger pointed outward. I don't have a lot of patience for these types of people. To me, it's clear: good leaders in any field, industry, department, company, or job make choices with integrity. They're reliable. They care about their reputation, not in terms of fame or money or even talent, but related to questions like "Am I trusted? Am I reliable? Am I fair? Do my words match my actions? Do I do the right things, even when they are hard?"

Luckily accountability is a skill you can hone. You can make a mental note of the ways in which you want to stay accountable—which could be as simple as showing up to meetings on time more regularly or responding to text messages within twenty-four hours—or be more public by telling friends or family members about more significant efforts, like following through on promises. This week think about what you accomplished (or didn't) as well as how you chose to spend your time, and see which parts align with your values and goals with respect to integrity (or not).

MAKE INTEGRITY THE DEFAULT CHOICE

Certain platitudes are drilled into your head as a kid, and one that sticks out in my brain is "It's not easy to do the right thing" concept. My parents repeatedly told my sisters and me that doing the right thing would feel exceptionally difficult almost every single time, and now as an adult, I understand their eagerness to properly set up expectations. Because, yeah, integrity is tough. Doing the right thing kind of sucks sometimes, or at least it might make you feel unsure, lousy, confused, criticized, and much more. It's much easier to play the victim card, feel entitled, and make an excuse; taking ownership for yourself and being accountable to your own integrity require a moral fiber and a willingness to try to make the right choice every single time while knowing you'll likely fail. Still, the work is worth it—and you have the power to make that decision.

A few years ago, a group of researchers at Harvard and Yale attempted to determine whether our first instinct is to act selfishly or cooperatively. They studied decision-making frameworks based on intuition or automatic action, and reflection or conscious thought. The result? All evidence pointed to cooperation—this idea that human beings lean toward integrity at first impulse. Of course, that's clearly not the case for everyone, nor is it a consistent behavior for anyone, but it reinforces the fact that integrity can be constructed one choice at a time. One of the best ways to see if your choices match your integrity? Make a conscious effort to ask yourself that very question. Another easy way to check your integrity: imagine the interaction is being recorded or taped. Would you be proud of your words or actions? What you do when no one is watching speaks volumes.

TRY THIS

Finish the sentence "I'm someone who..." with a phrase related to your definition of integrity, and make that your touchstone. For instance, if your sense of integrity is tied to punctuality, a phrase like "I'm someone who shows up on time" might help you hold yourself accountable.

Now What?

We all joke about people who have it together, and gently berate ourselves when we don't. But the truth is that nobody has their act together, not 100 percent of the time. And that's okay. I wrote this book for you—a regular person trying to juggle a thousand balls in the air with patience and purpose. Who sees glossy perfection everywhere and wonders how, or if, you'll ever measure up. Who occasionally feels out of control and wishes there was something you could *do* to create better, more sustainable habits. Who worries about falling short, even when it comes to self-care.

I've been there too. Heck, I'm still there, some days. Yet, I believe you're capable of creating a life you're proud of. My hope is that *you* believe you are too.

So here's a mini-manifesto of sorts, straight from my heart to yours:

I want you to enjoy your mornings as much as your weekends. I want you to view leisure time as worthwhile, and experience a big belly laugh at least once a week. I want you to be present for your days: right here, right now, not in the tiny box of a screen. I want you to feel at peace with your truest self, however it evolves.

I want you to move in this world with good health and a sense of gratitude toward your mind and body. I want you to understand that discipline doesn't equal deprivation; you can cherish a piece of really good chocolate as much as a sweaty run. I want you to seek rest and nourish your needs.

I want you to build relationships on the push-pull of authenticity and fairness, foundation and adventure, empathy and confidence. I want you to appreciate the feeling of being heard, so you can gift that same feeling to everyone you encounter. I want you to receive help with open arms and offer forgiveness like a spoonful of grace. I want you to trust your intuition, even if you're not sure what it's saying.

I want you to be empowered by what you make, spend, and save. I want you to make clear-eyed financial decisions, without the heft of debt, so you can put your money where your mouth is: community, travel, retirement, a home—whatever is important to you.

I want you to aim full speed ahead without losing your balance. I want you to do the work but also welcome the insights of others. I want you to ask for what you deserve, learn what you don't know, and use your influence to make the world a slightly better place.

And I want you to believe you can do all of the above.

These challenges aren't intended to highlight all the ways you're falling behind. They're available as a launchpad for igniting change in your life when you need it. Reach for this book whenever you're trying to get your life together...ish. I'm here for you every step of the way.

Index